Use of English

Use of English

Grammar practice activities for intermediate and upper-intermediate students

Student's Book

Leo Jones

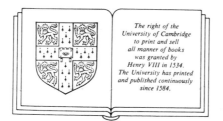

The right of the
University of Cambridge
to print and sell
all manner of books
was granted by
Henry VIII in 1534.
The University has printed
and published continuously
since 1584.

Cambridge University Press
Cambridge
New York   Port Chester
Melbourne   Sydney

Published by the Press Syndicate of the University of Cambridge
The Pitt Building, Trumpington Street, Cambridge CB2 1RP
40 West 20th Street, New York, NY 10011, USA
10 Stamford Road, Oakleigh, Melbourne 3166, Australia

© Cambridge University Press 1985

First published 1985
Seventh printing 1990

Printed in Great Britain
at the University Press, Cambridge

ISBN 0 521 26976 8 Student's Book
ISBN 0 521 26977 6 Teacher's Book

MX

Contents

To the student

Use of English is a book of activities and exercises for intermediate and upper-intermediate students who still make grammatical errors, who aren't fully confident about using English and who need to improve their accuracy in speech and in writing.

The exercises in this book will help you to:
- use English more confidently and fluently
- speak and write more accurately
- make fewer mistakes
- revise English grammar in an entertaining and interesting way
- learn how to express your ideas more exactly
- develop the ability to correct your own mistakes and depend less on having a teacher with you to help you all the time.

You'll be doing many of the exercises in groups or in pairs, so that everyone in the class has an equal chance to speak, express their ideas and share their opinions. While this is happening, your teacher can't be everywhere at the same time and correct all the mistakes everyone makes. This means that *you* must pay attention to what your partners are saying and be ready to suggest corrections. There's no need to correct every little error you notice, only the ones that are *relevant* to the exercise you're doing: these are mistakes connected with the theme of the unit.

You can't be *taught* to speak and write better English, you have to *learn* it. It's what you want to learn that you'll remember and not what I have written down in this book and not what your teacher tells you. You are the one who has the most important part to play in the learning process. If you want to know whether something is correct, or the meaning of a word or a better way of saying something, then it's up to you to find out – by asking your teacher, using a dictionary or by asking one of your partners.

Because many of the exercises are communicative, you'll probably find that many of them are more open-ended and less controlled than the grammar exercises or drills you've done before. In English – as in any language – there is rarely just *one* correct way of saying something. So, use the freedom you're given in the exercises to experiment with English and to find the words and structures that best express your *own* ideas and beliefs!

Activities shown with the symbol ✎ should be done in writing. Your teacher will tell you whether you should do these with a partner or alone in class, or as homework.

Activities shown with the symbol ♟ are communication activities, where you and a partner are given different information which you must communicate to each other. This information is given in 57 different sections at the end of the book, starting on page 99.

There are Grammar summaries which show the main points covered in each unit, starting on page 82. These are for you to use for reference and for revision.

1 QUESTIONS: *Wh-* and *Yes/No* questions

Space invader

1 What questions are the reporters asking? What answers do you think the space invader might give?

2 Work in pairs. Decide what questions the reporters are asking in each of the interviews below. Write down your best questions. Then give your list of questions to another pair to answer.

3 Role-play the interviews with a different partner.

It's not very clear

Work in pairs. Each of these photos is out of focus, as you can see. If one of you looks at communication activity 1 and the other at activity 6, you'll see the original photos which are clear and in focus. But *don't look* at each other's photos! Ask each other questions to find out more about each of the photos. (Activity 1 is on p.99, activity 6 on p.101.)

Yes or No?

Work in pairs. Think of three or four famous people, living or dead. Ask your partner questions to find out who each of the people he or she has in mind are.

The only answers your partner can give are: *Yes* or *Yes, in a way*
                                       No or *Not exactly*

I'd like to know...

I'd like to know...   ...how old you are.
Could you tell me...   ...when you were born?
Would you mind telling me ... what you enjoy doing?

1 Why isn't the interviewer asking simply: *How old are you?*
                                           When were you born?
                                           What do you enjoy doing?
Write down five more questions the polite young interviewer might ask.

2 Imagine you're an inexperienced young reporter interviewing a famous politician or entertainer. Role-play the interview with a partner, being as polite as possible to the great man or woman.

Where were you on the night of 13 May?

Complete the questions in this interrogation in writing.

Detective: Where ....

Suspect: At the cinema.

Detective: What ....

Suspect: I don't remember the name, I'm afraid.

Detective: When ....

Suspect: Oh, about 11 o'clock, I suppose.

Detective: Who ....

Suspect: No one, I went alone.

Detective: Where ....

Suspect: I went straight home then.

Detective: What ....

Suspect: At midnight.

What other questions might the detective have asked, do you think?

2 QUESTIONS: *Isn't it* questions

Making sure

Didn't we meet at Bruce's party?
Wasn't it Bruce who introduced us?
Aren't you the one who plays the piano?

Haven't you changed your hairstyle?
.... you use to have long hair?
.... you wearing a blue pullover?
.... your car damaged or something?
.... you have to leave suddenly?

Didn't you go to the cinema?

1 Find out quickly from your partner what he or she did on each day last week. Try to remember what you're told.

2 Separate from your partner and make brief notes of what you found out.

3 Talk to your partner again and make sure your notes were correct.
   Your conversation might begin like this:
   A: Didn't you go to the cinema on Sunday afternoon?
   B: No, that was Monday. Didn't you play tennis on Monday morning?
   A: That's right and didn't you...?

Finding out

You didn't come here by bus, *did you?*
You came in a flying saucer, *didn't you?*
You come from outer space, ...
That isn't very near here, ...
It was a long, tiring journey, ...
We look different from each other, ...
You've got three eyes, ...
You're not wearing a hat, ...
There's no hair on your head, ...
You can understand what I say, ...
I'm speaking slowly enough for you, ...
You'll come and have some tea with me, ...

Getting agreement

1 Begin by filling in the missing information below. Work alone.

The capital of the USA is	The opposite of *asleep* is ....
Queen Victoria reigned in the .... century.	You can't enter the UK without a ....
We're not allowed to .... in this room.	Yesterday was ....
Snakes, lizards and crocodiles are	All cats like to ....
The nicest country in the world is	The lesson ends at ....
Our teacher comes from	Computers weren't common until ....
Wonderful means the same as	Learning English is ....

2 Now work with a partner and make sure the information you've given agrees
with your partner's ideas. Your conversation might begin like this:
A: Washington's the capital of the USA, isn't it?
B: Yes, and the opposite of asleep is...

Your favourite colour's red, isn't it?   ▨

Work in groups of three. One of you should look at communication activity 3,
another at 9, and the third at 12. These are all at the back of the book. You'll be
finding out some personal information about each other.

You're John Brown, aren't you?   ▱

Fill in the gaps in this conversation.

Interviewer: Good morning. .... ?
Brown: No, I'm James Brown, not John Brown.

Interviewer: I see, ... ?
Brown: No, I've come about the job as a mechanic, not salesman.

Interviewer: Mechanic, eh? .... ?
Brown: No, actually I saw the advertisement in the Times, not the Echo.

Interviewer: The Times? Well, well. .... ?
Brown: No, my present employers are Acme Engineering.

Interviewer: Good firm! .... ?
Brown: No, they're the ones in Castle Lane, not Tower Street.

Interviewer: Of course. .... ?
Brown: Yes, I have. For just over three years now.
Interviewer: Good, good. Tell me about yourself, Mr.. er.. Mr...

3 THE PAST: What happened?

Have you ever...?

Have you ever ridden a horse?
Yes I have.
When was that?
I rode a horse last summer.
What was it like?
Oh, terribly difficult.
Why, what happened?
I fell off and hurt my foot.
What about you, have you ever ... ?

Work in pairs. One of you should look at communication activity 5 while the other looks at activity 15. You'll find both of these at the back of the book. You'll be finding out about some of your partner's achievements.

go – went – gone

1 Work in pairs. Fill in the gaps in this table of verb forms:

	beat		lay		
bite		bitten		lay	
		blown		lied	
choose				led	
	dealt			left	
drive			live		
eat			lose		
		flown		rose	
feel			steal		
	fell				torn
	hid				thrown
		held	wear		

2 Write sentences using the 10 verbs you found most difficult to remember.
  Use each one in *three* different ways, like this:
    She often loses her temper.   He sometimes feels embarrassed.
    He lost his way in the dark.   She felt something cold and slimy crawling up her leg.
    I've lost my front door key.   Have you ever felt lonely?

Famous men

Work in pairs. One of you should look at activity 18 while the other looks at activity 26. You will be talking about some famous people of the past who are well-known all over the world.

'My life'

1 Work in pairs. Find out about each year of your partner's life. Start with last year, then the year before that, and so on until you get back to the year he or she was born. Like this:
   A: How old were you in 1984?
   B: I was 24.
   A: And what happened to you in that year/when you were 24?
   B: I moved to a new flat and I changed my job. What about you? How old were you in 1984?

2 Form a pair with a different partner. Tell your new partner what you discovered about your first partner's life, but this time begin at the *beginning* of your previous partner's life.

One fine day...

Work in small groups. This cartoon strip has been printed in the wrong sequence. Can you rearrange the pictures to make a complete story? When you've done this, tell your group's version of the story to a member of a different group. Then write the story.

4 THE PAST: What was happening?

What were you doing?

1 What answers did the man give, do you think?
What's the difference in meaning between each of the sentences below?

She was having dinner when her husband came home.
She had dinner when her husband came home.
She had had dinner when her husband came home.

He went to the shops when the sun came out.
He'd been to the shops when the sun came out.
He was going to the shops when the sun came out.

2 Fill in the gaps in these sentences:

He .... three cups of coffee when I arrived.
She .... the door when she found her key.
I .... along slowly when a dog ran into the road.
He .... nearly half the book when he fell asleep.
He .... the baby when his wife got home.
I .... a cup of tea when the doorbell rang.

Yesterday

1 Fill in the gaps below showing what time you did the things listed.

Yesterday I got up at ...., started breakfast at .... and finished at ....
I left home at ...., went to .... and arrived there at ....
During the morning I .... and ....
I started lunch at .... and finished at ....
After lunch I .... and ....
I arrived home again at .... and had a meal from .... to ....
After eating I .... and then ....
Finally I went to bed at .... and fell asleep at ....

2 Work in pairs or small groups. Find out from each other what your partner(s) were doing at each of the times you've noted above. Your conversation might begin like this:

A: What were you doing at 7 o'clock yesterday morning?
B: I was still asleep. What about you?
A: Oh, I got up at 7 and had breakfast at about 7.30.
B: I was still lying in bed then. I didn't get up till after 8.

When the phone rang...

Write sentences describing what was going on when each of the events below happened. Use the words in italics in each sentence. Look at the example first:

When the phone rang ...   *window/view*
When the phone rang, I was looking out of the window admiring the view.
When the doorbell rang ...   *home/TV*
When the lights went out...   *armchair/book*
When the alarm clock went off...   *bed/summer holidays*
When my guests arrived...   *kitchen/meal*
When I met my old friend...   *park/flowers*
When the rain started...   *beach/sunshine*
When they called me for lunch...   *desk/working*

I opened the curtains and...

Imagine that this was the view from your window when you got up this morning. Write a paragraph describing what was going on outside at the time.

5 PAST, PRESENT AND FUTURE

A woman alone

Work in small groups. Look at the picture and decide together
- what has just happened
- what is going to happen next.

What's going on?

Work in pairs. One of you should look at activity 22 while the other looks at 32.
You'll be looking at a scene which you'll have to describe.

What's happened?

What do you think has happened to each of the people shown here? And what
do you think is going to happen next?

Those were the days

Do you still go jogging?
Didn't you use to smoke heavily?

I don't smoke any more.
I used to see a lot of Mary.
I haven't seen her since 1980.
I haven't had a beard for four years.

Work in pairs. Imagine that you're two old friends who haven't seen each other for five years. Talk about the following activities you used to do:

A

play the piano	drink milk shakes
go running	go to the theatre
be a teacher	play tennis
go out with Pat	ride a racing bike
listen to rock music	have private
spend holidays in Florida	English lessons

B

play the guitar	drink Guinness
go for long walks	go to the cinema
be a civil servant	play basketball
go out with Viv	ride a motorbike
listen to classical music	attend English
spend holidays in Spain	classes

Before TV

What did people use to do before they had television?
How did they spend their free time?
How has TV changed people's lives?
Without TV, how would your own life be different?

1 Work in groups. Try answering similar questions about the following inventions and discoveries we now depend on:

planes	tape recorders	plastics	microchips
electric lights	cars	computers	vaccination

Think of some other inventions or discoveries we now take for granted.

2 Write a paragraph describing the most interesting points that were made in your group.

6 SPELLING AND PRONUNCIATION

What's in a name?

Edson Arantes do Nascimento   Norma Jean Baker   Michel Shalhouz

Work in pairs. One of you should look at activity 17 while the other looks at 21. Listen carefully while your partner spells some more unfamiliar names to you and write them down. See if you can guess who each person is better known as.

Did you say 'court' or 'caught'?

Each of the words below is pronounced the same as another familiar word with a different spelling. Can you find each word's 'twin'?

brake	meet	seen	wait
dew	nose	shore	waste
flew	right	steel	weather
guessed	root	tale	week
hole	peace	threw	wore

A E I O U

/iː/	/ɪ/	/æ/	/e/	/aː/	/ɒ/	/ʌ/	/ɔː/	/uː/	/ɜː/	/ʊ/
sheep	ship	man	men	march	collar	colour	caller	pool	pearl	pull
queen	which	match	head	laugh	cough	funny	short	lose	girl	book
ceiling	guilty	hand	says	drama	wash	flood	sure	true	turn	push

Work in pairs. One of you should look at activity 4 while the other looks at 20. You'll be dictating words to your partner and checking his or her spelling.

'ei' or 'ie'?

/iː/	/iː/	/eɪ/	/aɪ/	/e/	/ə/	/eə/
believe	ceiling	eight	die	friend	foreign	their
field	receive	beige	either	Leicester		heir
grief	deceive					

Choose the correct spelling of the words below and add them to the appropriate columns above:

height–hieght   receipt–reciept   leisure–liesure   seize–sieze   neighbour–nieghbour
theif–thief   releif–relief   weight–wieght   cheif–chief   neither–niether

Eh?.. Oh!.. Ow!

/eɪ/	/əʊ/	/aʊ/	/eə/	/aɪ/	/ɪə/	/ɔɪ/
Eh?	Oh!	Ow!	air	eye	ear	
tray	go	how	bear	high	beer	toy
bay	know	plough	share	buy	hear	boy
eight	comb	cow	hair	die	clear	point

Work in pairs. One of you should look at activity 10 while the other looks at 24.
You'll be dictating some more words to your partner.

Hoping or hopping?

Add -ing to each of these verbs, changing the spelling as necessary:

hope   hop   shop   travel   refer   begin   visit   let
upset   quarrel   run   keep   offer   fit   benefit   kidnap

Correct the mistakes

In the following story there are 20 spelling mistakes. Can you find them *and* correct them all?

Whenever I'm not smilling, people allways ask me wether I'm feelling
deppressed or just a mizerable sort of person. It's an awful nuisance
becase no one can walk round grining on every occasion and I don't
beleive that basicly other people are any happyer than me. Psycholgists
(or do I mean psychyatrists ?) would probabley say that I'm lieing to
myself but I sincerely believe it's true. Althrough I try to practice
smiling in front of the miror, it doesn't seem to have any affect. My
friends and aquaintances say, 'Come on, cheer up. It's not that bad!'

7 PUNCTUATION

Say it aloud

1 How would you say each of these punctuation marks aloud in English?

? ! . , : ; ' ( ) " " - —

2 Decide with a partner which of the sentences below are punctuated correctly and which contain mistakes.

Its' nice today, is'nt it?	It's nice today, isn't it?
Our cat's hurt its paw.	Our cats hurt it's paw.
He's a tall, dark, handsome man.	He's a tall dark handsome man.
She told me, that she was sixteen.	She told me that she was sixteen.
If you want to see him make an appointment.	If you want to see him, make an appointment.
Make an appointment if you want to see him.	Make an appointment, if you want to see him.
The person who phoned left this message.	The person, who phoned, left this message.
My mum, who is 62, never eats sweets.	My mum who is 62 never eats sweets.
My dad, on the other hand, has a sweet tooth.	My dad on the other hand has a sweet tooth.
That's right! he said. "That's right!" he said.	"That's right," he said.

Excuse me, please.

Rewrite this dialogue, putting in the correct punctuation.

Man: Excuse me please
Woman: Yes can I help you sir
Man: Id like to know when the Paris flight gets here
Woman: Which flight do you mean the British Airways flight or the Air France one
Man: Its the British Airways I think because the flight number is BA 144
Woman: OK Ill check for you if youd just wait a moment Yes the scheduled arrival time is 1900 but theres a delay of 30 minutes
Man: Oh I see fine thank you Is there likely to be any further delay do you think
Woman: No the planes already on its way so unless theres a headwind or something its probably going to land at about 1930
Man: Right thanks very much for your help
Woman: Youre welcome sir Goodbye
Man: Bye

14

etc.

Many abbreviations in modern English can be written with or without full stops. This means we can write:

e.g. or eg (= for example)
i.e. or ie (= that is)

The abbreviations in the table below are printed in the way you're most likely to see them written. What do they all mean? See if the members of your group know.

am	St	max.	VAT	BBC
pm	Rd	min.	LP	EEC
mph	Ave	approx.	UN	HQ
b & b	Sq.	intro.	UK	GMT
h & c	Dept	tel.	CUP	PTO

CAPITAL LETTERS

All the words in the sentences below are written with small letters. Change them, where necessary, into capitals.

I'll see you on friday or at the weekend, mr jones.
If we don't meet in the summer, let's meet in september or at christmas.
This is uncle ted who's in the royal air force.
I saw a programme about the sun and the moon on tv last night.
Most scottish people prefer to call themselves scots – unlike the whisky
    which is always called scotch. And the hq of the metropolitan police is
    called scotland yard, which is in london.
Now that he's a doctor, the name plate on his door says 'dr swan'.

Dear Mr Brown,

Rearrange the layout, punctuation and capital letters in this letter.

108 alma road bournemouth bh9 1al
14 april 1985
dear mr brown
Im writing to you to let you know that Ill be away from school until monday next
Im sorry I couldnt let you know in person but your secretary told me you were busy
so I didnt want to disturb you
the reason for my absence is that my uncle from the united states is paying us
an unexpected visit and as Im the only one in the family who speaks english Im
going to have to look after him
if I had known sooner Id have told you but as I said the visit is unexpected
yours sincerely
maria garcia class b13

8 POSITION: Place

Mouse trouble

Mr Jones's house is full of mice. Can you explain *exactly* where each mouse is, without pointing at them? The expressions below may be useful.

in front of
in the middle of
by the side of
at the back of
on the edge of
in the corner of
at the top of

Where are the mistakes?

1 Before you try the exercise, look at Mr Jones's garden shed and notice where each of his children are standing!

2 Now look at the newspaper article below and find all the misprints and punctuation errors. Then explain exactly where each one is. There are 25 mistakes altogether.

School Boss Stole From Funds

Over a period of eight yaers the owner of a language school took over £220,000 from the school + funds to provide himself with a life of luxury.

Yesterday he went to jail for 3 three years.

Australian-born Samuel Bates, 47, took over as managing director of the National Language Institute Institute in Beckenham in 1907.

As well as a normal bank account for the school in Beckenham, , there was a personal account and a sch-school account at the Bank of New Zealand $ in the City of London, the court was told ½

Mr James O,Connor, prosecuting, told hte court that Bates put through just enough money in the Beckenham account to cover expences. The rest of the the school fees went into another school account which Bates later transferred into his own account ?

Mr O'Connor said that the money which Bates stole was useD for 'extravagant personal luxuries'.

Bates, of east street in Beckenham, claimed that he was haveing 'problems' iwht with the tax people' and that he had not intended to to steal money from the school.

The judge, Mr Justice McInnes, sentences Bates to four years in jail and called him 'a nasty and called him 'a nasty little man'.

16

Where shall I put A?

Work in pairs. One of you should use letters A to M, the other N to Z. Put your 13 letters in different places on this map, but don't let your partner see. Then, find out from your partner where to put each of his or her letters on your map. Insist on getting *exact* instructions.

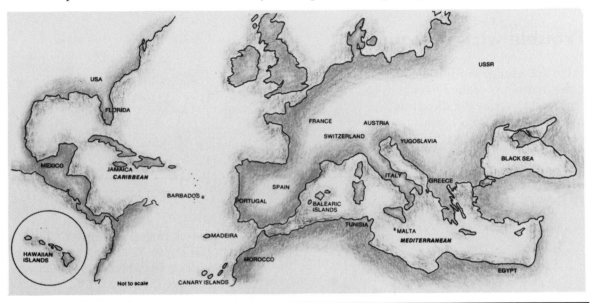

What does it look like?

Work in pairs. One of you should look at activity 14 while the other looks at 27. You'll have to draw something as your partner describes it, so have a pencil and paper ready.

Fill in the gaps

Fill each gap in the passage with a suitable word or phrase.

So there I was, standing alone .... the mountain looking .... the view. I was .... by snow-capped peaks and could see the sun starting to set .... Slowly a red glow spread .... the sky, making the .... peaks look pink, until the sun finally dropped .... the horizon. Soon it would be quite dark and I could see grey clouds .... and could feel a chill .... the air. It would have been foolish to stay .... much longer and I started walking .... the slope towards the mountain hotel, which was half an hour's walk .... I was going to spend the night .... Sure enough, it began to snow and I realised that the path .... the rocks would soon be .... I started to run, not wanting to get lost .... the mountain. I stopped .... a tree for a moment and saw the hotel .... me. Of course I got there easily, but the next day the snow was so .... that we all stayed ...., singing songs .... the fire.

9 POSITION: Direction and motion

Trouble with mosquitoes

There are a lot of mosquitoes in the bedrooms of the Hotel Tropical! Describe the direction that each mosquito is flying in, from the point of view of the sleepless hotel guest.

Where did it go?

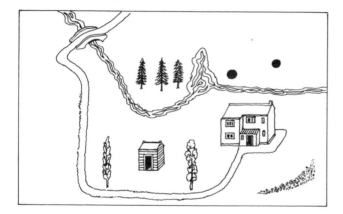

Some kind of animal got into Mr Jones's garden last night. Your teacher is going to explain exactly where it went. Draw the exact route the animal took on the plan on the left. What kind of animal was it, do you think?

Go straight on until...

Work in pairs. One of you should look at activity 11, and the other at 57. You're going to describe a route to your partner.

1	2	3	4	5	6	7	8	9	10
11	12	13	14	15	16	17	18	19	20
21	22	23	24	25	26	27	28	29	30
31	32	33	34	35	36	37	●	39	40
41	42	43	44	45	46	47	48	49	50
51	52	53	54	55	56	57	58	59	60
61	62	63	64	65	66	67	68	69	70
71	72	73	74	75	76	77	78	79	80
81	82	83	84	85	86	87	88	89	90
91	92	93	94	95	96	97	98	99	100

This way please!

Imagine that you are taking an elderly relative on a sightseeing visit to downtown Toronto. Your relative wants to see *all* the sights shown on this map but can't walk very far. Work out the shortest possible route.

❶ Union Station
❷ Harbourfront (leisure area)
❸ C. N. Tower (panoramic views)
❹ Toronto Dominion Centre (underground shopping centre)
❺ Art Gallery of Ontario
❻ City Hall
❼ Toronto Eaton Centre (shopping centre)
❽ St Michael's Cathedral
❾ St James Cathedral
❿ St Lawrence Market
⓫ Toronto Island Ferry Terminal

Run, walk or fly

1 How many different verbs can you think of to describe ways of going or moving somewhere? Make a list, beginning like this:

   run, walk, fly, fall, cycle, ...

2 Now use the verbs in your list to make sentences about each scene below. Use one of these words in each sentence:

   across   away   (a)round   past   over   along   in   out   up and down
   For example: 'The stream was quite narrow and we were able to jump over.'

19

10 DOING THINGS: Requests and obligation

Would you mind...?

Would you mind...?   No, of course not.
Could you...?   Yes, of course.
Can you ... please? Certainly.

Would you mind if I...? Not at all.
Do you mind if I...?   No, of course not.
May I...?   Yes, of course.
Is it all right if I...?   By all means.
Could I...?   Certainly.

What would you say to someone if...

the door was locked?	the room was too dark?
you were hungry?	your suitcase was too heavy?
you felt tired?	you couldn't do your homework?
you felt cold?	you wanted to make a phone call?
you needed a dictionary?	you felt hot and sweaty?

I'd like you to...

I'd like you to...
I want you to...
Can you...?
Please will you...?

All right.
OK.
Right.
Sure.

Work in pairs. One of you should look at activity 8 while the other looks at 19. You'll be telling your partner to do various things, using the expressions above.

Make yourself at home?

Imagine that a very easy-going friend is coming to stay at your parents' house and that they are very strict about tidiness, punctuality, smoking, etc. What can your friend do and what can't he or she do there? Work in small groups. (If you're living with a landlady, imagine a very strict landlady instead.)

Complete each of these sentences with advice for your friend:

You can...	It's all right to...	You can't...	You mustn't...
You're allowed to...	If you like you can...	You aren't supposed to...	You aren't allowed to...

Enjoy your flight!

1 Work in groups. Decide together which of the following things can be taken onto a plane free of charge, in addition to one piece of hand luggage.

umbrella	skis	small dog	walking stick	magazines
binoculars	baby food	baby's carrycot	small camera	books
overcoat	briefcase	child's pushchair	lady's handbag	sandwiches

2 And decide which of the following activities are permitted or forbidden on board an aircraft.

drinking	smoking	opening doors and windows
eating	standing up	undoing seat belt
running	sleeping	walking about

3 Look at communication activity 7 to see if you were right.

Do I have to...?

> Do I have to...
> Is it necessary to...?
> Ought I to...?
> Have I got to...?

> You don't have to...   You have to...
> You needn't...   You've got to...
> There's no need to...   You ought to...
> You haven't got to...   It's wise to...

Imagine that you're talking to a foreigner who is going to visit your country for the very first time. Try to put yourself in a foreigner's shoes and imagine what would be *different* about life in your country. What advice would you give about the laws and habits he or she would have to get used to? For example, what about:

crossing the frontier: passport, customs, visa, vaccination certificate, etc.
transport: using taxis, public transport, driving a car, etc.
shopping and eating: behaviour in shops, restaurants, cafes, etc.
social behaviour: meeting strangers, visiting people at home, etc.
language difficulties: using English, your own language, dialect problems, etc.

In other words

Each of the sentences below can be rewritten using the openings given.

In class you mustn't chew gum.	You aren't ....
Is it necessary to attend every lesson?	Do I ....
Can I bring my pet dog into class?	Is ....
Open your books at page 13.	I ....
You don't have to wear a suit.	There ....
Could I leave early today?	Would ....
Could you give these books out?	Would ....
Exams are not compulsory.	You don't ....

11 DOING THINGS: Ability

Evening classes

Imagine that you decided to enrol in each of the evening classes advertised on the left:
> What would you say before you enrolled?
> What would you think during the first lesson?
> What would you be able to say proudly at the end of the course?

Shopping lists

Work in pairs. One of you should look at activity 2 while the other looks at 13. You'll be talking about the items on your shopping lists you were able or unable to get.

12 eggs (size 3)
1 kg carrots
3 large tins beans
1 jar marmalade
2 small wholemeal loaves
2 packets chocolate biscuits
1 jar instant coffee

1 large roll sticky tape
1 box paper clips
2 cassettes (C 90)
2 red ballpoints
4 size AA alkaline batteries
1 packet airmail envelopes
1 large glue stick

Success at last!

She managed to...   *He didn't manage to...*
She succeeded in ...-ing ...   *He didn't succeed in ...-ing ...*
She was able to...   *He wasn't able to...*
    He couldn't...

1 Write sentences about the scenes shown in the cartoons, using the structures above. For example: 'He didn't succeed in opening the door'.

2 Think of three things *you* have succeeded in doing recently and three things you tried to do but didn't manage to do successfully.

Do-it-yourself?

How well can you survive without 'experts' to help you? Which of the jobs shown here can you do without help? Be honest! Use the phrases below to tell your partners about your own abilities.

I can do that myself.
I'd need someone to help me.
I'd get someone to help me do that.
I'd have that done for me.
I'd get ... to do that for me.
I don't know how to...

paint a ceiling	service a car
fit an electric plug	change the wheel
fix new shelves	on a car
replace a fuse	sew on a button
change a light bulb	iron a shirt
wallpaper a room	bake a cake
install central	lay a carpet
heating	fix a broken TV
replace a broken	repair a cassette
window pane	type a letter

In other words

Rewrite each of these sentences, using the words in capitals on the left.

MANAGE   He was able to swim to the river bank safely.
UNABLE   They couldn't get out of the country.
SUCCEED   She was able to finish her work in time.
MANAGE   He couldn't get away from the police.
CAPABLE   She can play any tune on the piano by ear.
COULD   She was unable to understand what I meant.
GET   She had the wedding cake made by her mother.
NEED   Only a very good mechanic could repair your car.
HAVE   My hair is going to be cut tomorrow.

12 DOING THINGS: Advice and suggestions

What should I do?

What should I do?
Would it be a good idea to...?
Should I ... or ... ?
Is it worth...?
Is there any point in ...?
I can't decide whether to ... or ...
I can't make up my mind whether to ... or ...
I'm wondering whether to ... or ...

What do you think I should do?
Do you think it would be a good idea to...?
Do you think I should ... or ... ?
Do you think it's worth...?
Do you think there's any point in...?

Work in pairs. Make up sentences using the expressions above and write them down. Here are some ideas to start you off:
    You don't know where to go on holiday.
    Should you travel by plane or sea?
    Is it best to buy a new car or a second-hand one?
    This evening you could watch TV or go out.
    You could buy the book or borrow it from the library.
    You could get your hair cut or let it grow.

If I were you...

What advice would you give to Joe using the expressions below?
If I were you ...   *My advice would be to ...*
I think you ought to ...   *It'd be best to ...*
Why don't you ...   *You'd better ...*
I'd advise you to ...   *It's time you ...*

There's no point in ...

Imagine that a good friend of yours is having a bad time at work and is thinking of leaving and looking for another job elsewhere. You think it's unwise to leave a good job. What would you say to your friend using these expressions?

I don't think you ought to ...   *There's no point in ...*
It isn't a good idea to ...   *It'd be better not to ...*
I wouldn't advise you to ...   *If I were you I wouldn't ...*

Suppose another friend was thinking of doing the following things, what advice would you give?

swimming from England to France   opening a vegetarian restaurant
taking up hang-gliding   buying a video recorder
writing an autobiography   going to the USA next winter
getting married   becoming a teacher

That's easier said than done

Work in groups of four. Each member of the group should play the role of one of these people and ask the others for advice. You can reject unsuitable advice by saying:

That's easier said than done, because...   or   *I don't think that would work because...*

People with problems

Write a suitable reply to one of these letters. Imagine that they were sent to you by friends.

and I've become so dependent on them that I can't give them up. Yesterday I got through 3 whole packets! I've just got no willpower, as you know.
What do you think I should do?
Love,
Liz

and my boss wants me to move to New York and take over our American branch. This would mean leaving all my friends and starting a new life. Perhaps I should tell him I'm not interested in promotion? What do you think?
Yours
Bob.

13 VERB + VERB: *-ing* and *to* . . .

It's easy to...

1 Fill in the gaps in the sentences below, so that the meaning of each pair of sentences is the same as the one above.

I can easily write a 150-word composition.

<u>Writing a 150-word composition</u> is easy.   It's simple <u>to write a 150-word composition.</u>

I like going abroad on holiday.

.... is lovely.   It's nice ....

I get embarrassed when I have to meet strangers.

.... is embarrassing.   It's embarrassing for me ....

I can only run round the block with difficulty.

.... is difficult.   It's hard ....

I can't stand it when I'm criticised.

.... is awful.   It's horrible ....

2 Now write some more sentences using the same adjectives, but this time about your *own* feelings and opinions.

Without blinking

Can you keep your eyes open for a whole minute without blinking once?

Complete the sentences in a suitable way:

Can you sneeze without ....
Can you stop hiccups by ....
Can you cure a cold by ....

Can you write a letter in English without ....
Can you touch your toes without ....
Can you stand on one leg while ....

-ing or *to*... ?

Study the verbs in the lists here before doing the exercises opposite.

<u>VERBS + -ing:</u> *avoid   carry on   detest   dislike   enjoy   finish   give up   can't help   keep on   mind   miss   put off   risk   can't stand*

<u>VERBS + to ... :</u> *can't afford   choose   dare   expect   fail   happen   hesitate   learn   manage   mean   need   prepare   pretend   wait*

26

In other words

Rewrite each sentence using the word on the left.

PRETEND   He was wearing a policeman's uniform.
AFFORD   That new TV is too expensive for us to buy.
DISLIKE   I'm not fond of watching TV every evening.
PUT OFF   I'm going to write some letters tomorrow, not today.
RISK   You shouldn't go swimming here in case you drown.
HESITATE   I don't want to criticise your performance.
FAIL   The parcel didn't arrive.
WAIT   I'm sitting here until the doctor arrives.
GIVE UP   Smoking is bad for your health, you know.

I prefer...

1 Look at the verbs in this list. They can all be used with *-ing* or with *to* ... without changing the meaning very much. You may prefer to use the forms you feel most comfortable with.

begin	*intend*	*prefer*
continue	*like*	*propose*
hate	*love*	*start*

2 Rewrite each of these sentences using the verbs on the left.

LOVE   He thinks football is a wonderful game to play.
START   He waited for the referee's whistle and then kicked off.
HATE   He doesn't enjoy washing up one little bit!
INTEND   I've booked a holiday in Spain for the week after Easter.
BEGIN   She felt better soon after taking her medicine.

3 What things do you love, like or hate doing (*or* to do)? And what do you enjoy or dislike doing? Tell your partner(s).

Finish the sentences

Their dog is so fierce that I'd never dare ...
After answering the phone he continued ...
I've got such a bad cold that I can't help ...
Please carry on working, I really don't mind ...
While she's so far away from home she misses ...
I dislike Bill so much that I always try to avoid ...
While I was in town the day before yesterday I happened ...
During the next twelve months I expect ...

14 VERB + VERB: *-ing, to . . .* and *that . . .*

He seems to ...

It seems that he likes animals.
He seems to like animals.

It seems that he is feeling happy.
He seems to be feeling happy.

It seems that he has been robbed.
He seems to have been robbed.

It seems that he has lost his money.
He seems to have lost his money.

Rewrite each sentence, starting with the phrase on the right.

It appears that the window is broken.   The window appears ...
It seems that some of my books are missing.   Some of my books seem ...
It seems that none of my records have been touched.   None of my records seem ...
It appears that nobody heard any suspicious noises.   Nobody appears ...
It is thought that the thief is someone I know.   The thief is thought ...
It is believed that he knows me quite well.   He is believed ...

---

to ... or *that ...* ?

Study the verbs in the lists below before trying the exercises opposite.

VERB + OBJECT + to ...
He taught me to speak
Japanese.

encourage	help
force	invite
get	teach

VERB + to ... or + that ...
He pretended to be a ghost or
He pretended that he was a ghost.

decide	hope
pretend	expect

VERB + that ...
I heard that she was in Paris or *I heard she was in Paris.*

assume	deny	find out	realise
believe	doubt	guess	suppose
bet	dream	hear	think
consider	feel	know	understand

In other words

Rewrite each sentence using the verb on the left.

THINK   According to him, all strikers should be thrown into jail.
INVITE   She asked me if I wanted to go dancing with her.
FIND OUT He received a letter telling him that he hadn't got the job.
BET   It's impossible for you to guess the answer.
·HOPE   With any luck I'll see you again in the spring.
DREAM   I was being chased down a long corridor by a monster.
FORCE   Their parents said they had to go to bed early.
GET   He asked his secretary to make the call for him.
FEEL   I got the impression that she didn't really like me.
KNOW   There's no chance of her coming to see us today.

While I was out...

I noticed someone looking over the wall.
I noticed that someone was looking over the wall.

Now listen, Timmy, Oliver, Daniel, Thomas and Jeremy, while I'm out you
mustn't paint on the wall, play in my room, spill drinks on the carpet,
use my typewriter or go into the kitchen. All right?

Finish the sentences below to describe what the naughty children did:

While I was out I imagined...
When I got home I found...
And then I discovered...
And noticed...
And believe it or not, I caught*...

(*catch can only be used like this: *The farmer caught us stealing his apples.*)

Finish the sentences

You've won first prize? But I never realised ...
I can't find my keys. Will you please help ...
I think she'd succeed if someone encouraged ...
What a lovely surprise! I didn't expect ...
While you were sitting in the garden did you notice ...
As soon as I heard the phone ring I guessed ...
After a long discussion they decided ...
He's such a bad teacher he couldn't teach ...

15 VERB + VERB: *-ing* or *to* . . .?

Stop!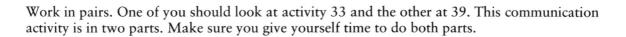

Work in pairs. One of you should look at activity 33 and the other at 39. This communication activity is in two parts. Make sure you give yourself time to do both parts.

Don't forget!

I'm terribly sorry but I've forgotten to bring my wallet. I remember seeing it on the hall table earlier but I didn't remember to bring it with me. Sorry!

Work in pairs again. One of you should look at activity 38 and the other at 47. Again make sure that you give yourselves time to do both parts of this activity.

Looking forward to ...

I'm not looking forward to getting up early.

1 Work in small groups. Imagine that you're giving advice to a young friend who is about to start his or her first job:
   What do you think your friend is looking forward to doing?
   What do you think he or she is *not* looking forward to?
   What will your friend have to get used or accustomed to doing?
   What do you think your friend may object to doing?
2 Write down the five best pieces of advice your group has thought of.

Sorry!

He's sorry about letting the plant die.
And she's sorry that it's dead.

Complete the unfinished sentences:

She apologised for breaking his new glasses.
   (She's sorry ...   And he's sorry ...   )
I'm sorry to have to tell you that I've lost your money.
   (I'm sorry ...   And you're sorry ...   )
He was so nervous that he spilt coffee all over her new dress.
   (He was sorry ...   And she was sorry ...   )
   (So he apologised ...   )

I'M SORRY TO TELL YOU THIS BUT YOUR FICUS ELASTICA HAS DIED.

Rules

Smoking isn't allowed!

I wish they'd let us smoke.

Yes, it's a pity we aren't allowed to smoke.

· NO SMOKING ·

SCHOOL RULES: No smoking
singing
dancing
shouting
swearing
fighting
cheating

SHOW RESPECT TO TEACHERS
ARRIVE NO LATER THAN 8·55
ALWAYS WRITE IN INK
SPEAK ONLY ENGLISH
SILENCE WHEN TEACHER IS TALKING
2 HOURS' HOMEWORK EVERY NIGHT

Write more sentences about the 'school rules' above, using these phrases:

We aren't allowed ...   *We're forced to ...*
They won't let us ...   *They make us ...*
... isn't allowed.   *... is compulsory.*

In other words

I wish you wouldn't ask so many questions. Please stop ....
NO PARKING IN SCHOOL GROUNDS. We aren't allowed ....
I think we need some petrol. We'd better stop ....
We used to play cards every evening. I'll never forget ....
I've drunk your coffee by mistake. I'm sorry ....
I get embarrassed when I meet strangers. I'm not used ....
I didn't tell you my phone number. I forgot ....
I cough when I smoke a cigarette. Cigarettes make ....

16 THE FUTURE: Plans and intentions

One day...

Complete each of the sentences in your own words:

One of these days I ....

Tomorrow morning at 9.15 I ....

What presents .... for your next birthday?

By the time the bus .... we'll all be wet through.

After work next Friday I ....

I'll .... when the bell rings.

Their plane .... at 6 o'clock tomorrow morning.

As soon as I can I ....

Reporting

How would you report each sentence, using the verbs shown?

'I won't* tell anyone about our secret.'

'I'm going to visit Italy next summer.'

'Will you help me to do this please?'

'I think you'll* enjoy reading this book.'

'Will* you be quiet!'

'I'm going to study hard for the exam.'

'I'll* hit you if you don't do what I say!'

'You'll* get cold if you forget your hat.'

'I'll open the door.'

'I'm going to open the door.'

'I'll make you a lovely birthday cake!'

(* *going to* can be used here, without much change in meaning.)

PROMISE	He promised not to tell anyone.
INTEND	He intends to visit Italy.
ASK	He asked me to ....
ADVISE	....
TELL	....
INTEND	....
THREATEN	....
WARN	....
OFFER	....
INTEND	....
OFFER	....

Correct the mistakes

There is an error in each sentence. Can you find it *and* correct it?

I'll make some tea when my friends will arrive.

The weather's getting better next week.

His sister will have a baby the month after next.

I think I go out for a walk soon.

If they're going to have enough money, they're going abroad this summer.

We won't catch the train if we won't hurry.

Consequences

What would you say if someone made these threats or statements?

'I'm going to drink two whole cartons of milk!'
'I'm going to drive flat out all the way there.'
'I'm going to hold my breath for ten minutes.'
'I'm not going to phone home this month.'
'I'm going to steal that old lady's handbag.'
'I'm not going to come to this class ever again.'
'I'm going to go on studying until my English is perfect.'

Planning ahead

	MON	TUE	WED	THUR	FRI	SAT	SUN
am							
pm							
evening							

1 Begin by filling in your own plans and appointments for each day next week.
   If necessary, add some imaginary plans.
2 Work in pairs. Find out what your partner is going to do each day. Then find
   out how the plans might change **if something unexpected happens**.
   For example:
      'What will you do if you're ill that morning?'
      'What will you do if the weather's bad that afternoon?'
   Some typical unforeseen events could be:
      strike   illness   bad weather   parents' visit   delay   accident

Next summer...

Fill each gap with suitable words or phrases:

1 Next summer I .... have a really good holiday. Of course, I .... have
   to save up for it and do without some luxuries because otherwise I .... able to
   afford it. I haven't decided where I .... go yet. On the one hand it ....
   nice to go somewhere warm and sunny where I .... lie on the beach all day, but
   on the other hand I .... get bored with that and it .... better to
   choose a more active holiday. The important thing .... have a real change from
   routine. While .... away, I .... send you a postcard!

2 What are *you* going to do during your next holidays? Tell your partner.

17 PROBABILITY

How sure are you?

DEFINITELY	*I'm (absolutely) sure it'll happen.* *I'm quite sure it'll happen.*	*It must be going to happen.* *It'll happen, that's for sure.* *It's sure to happen.*
PROBABLY	*It'll probably happen.* *I expect it'll happen.* *It may (or could) well happen.*	*It's likely to happen.* *It looks as if it'll happen.* *It seems to be going to happen.*
POSSIBLY	*It may happen.* *It could happen.* *It might happen.* *There's a chance it'll happen.*	
PROBABLY NOT	*It probably won't happen.* *I don't expect it'll happen.* *I doubt if it'll happen.*	*It's unlikely to happen.* *It doesn't look as if it'll happen.* *It doesn't seem to be going to happen.*
DEFINITELY NOT	*I'm absolutely sure it won't happen.* *I'm quite certain it won't happen.*	*It won't happen, that's for sure.* *It can't be going to happen.*

Use the expressions above to complete the sentences below. Work in small groups.

Before long children in schools ...
In a few years' time everyone ...
In the year 2000 spacecraft ...
By the time I'm 60 ...
This time tomorrow ...
When this course finishes ...
In the next Olympics my country's team ...

Looking on the bright side?

Work in pairs. One of you is an optimist, the other a pessimist. Discuss each situation.

34

Is it true?

All of the expressions in the list opposite can be used to say how sure you are that something is true or not. For example:

It's sure to be true.   *It can't be true.*
It could well be true.   *It seems to be true.*

1 Work in pairs. Write down *five* things about yourselves which are true and *five* things which are untrue (but which could be true).

2 Form a larger group and tell your new partners about the things on your list. Use the expressions opposite to say how firmly you believe what they tell you. Like this:
  A: B's parents both have red hair.
  C: That could well be true, don't you think, D?
  D: No, I doubt if that's true because B's own hair is very dark.

Did it happen?

1 What changes have to be made to the expressions opposite to talk about how certain you are about events that happened *in the past?* For example, we'd say:
  It's sure to have happened.   *It must have happened.*

2 What do you think has happened in each of the scenes shown here? Discuss them with your partner(s).

Why do you think ... ?   🔲

Work in pairs. One of you should look at activity 36 while the other looks at 41. You'll be guessing the causes of a number of events.

In other words   🔲

Rewrite each sentence so that its meaning remains unchanged.

I'm sure our train will be late.	Our train ....
I probably won't see you tomorrow.	I doubt ....
I'm sure I wasn't told about the party.	I ....
They seem to be a wonderfully happy couple.	I ....
It looks as if you've had a nasty shock.	You ....
This can't possibly be your handwriting.	This ....
You probably weren't careful enough.	It ....

18 COMPARISON

Braver than a lion!

1 Work in groups. Make a list of all the animals shown above in order of size, from the biggest down to the smallest.
2 Decide which of the animals shown is the:
   fastest   slowest   fiercest   most lovable   rarest   most common

---

More exciting than knitting!!

I think sewing is far more difficult than knitting!

Well, I think it's much less difficult.

Anyhow, neither of them is as difficult as learning English!

Work in groups. Try to come to some sort of agreement between you on each of the activities in the list below. Decide which is the:
   most exciting   dullest   most dangerous   safest
   most energetic   most restful   most rewarding   most mindless

bufferfly collecting	cooking	disco dancing	sewing
learning a foreign language	cycling	hang-gliding	skiing
watching television	knitting	mountain climbing	parachuting
playing the piano	reading	playing football	fishing
stamp collecting	walking	scuba diving	swimming

36

It's the most ...

Joe's the tallest.
Pete's the youngest.
Jim's the most intelligent.
Ted's the oldest.

Work in groups. What can you say about *each one* of the items grouped together below, using *the most...* or *the -est...*?

apple grapefruit pineapple lemon   bicycle motorbike train camel
Toronto Cambridge Athens Sao Paulo   wine beer brandy fruit juice
January April July (in your country)   Rolls Royce Ferrari VW Beetle Land Rover

---

It's much too big!

Work in small groups and write *four* sentences about each of the cartoons. For example:
The van isn't big enough for the elephant to get in.
The elephant's too big to get in the van.
An elephant is such a big animal that it won't fit in a van.
He's so big that we'll have to get a lorry.

In other words

It isn't as warm in Canada as it is in Mexico.   Mexico is a ....
Driving a car takes more skill than riding a bike.   It doesn't ....
No one I know is more arrogant than him.   He's ....
That's the nicest thing anyone's ever said to me.   No one has ....
I can't walk such a long way with my bad leg.   It's ....
A Boeing 747 holds more passengers than a DC-10.   A DC-10 ....
I prefer milk chocolate to plain chocolate.   I think milk ....
This shirt is too dirty for me to wear.   This shirt isn't ....

37

19 REPORTED SPEECH: Statements

What do you think?

He says that ...   *He thinks that ...*
According to him ...   *He believes that ...*
Apparently ...   *He feels that ...*

Stand up and go round the class, asking as many other students as possible what their opinions are about the topics below. Then, when you've done this, find a partner and report to him or her what you found out.

Not wearing a seat belt	Wearing a hat indoors	Watching TV in the morning
Cheating in an exam	Eating ice cream for breakfast	Not returning a borrowed book
Fiddling your expenses	Getting up at midday	Kicking a dog
Not paying your taxes	Going to bed at 3 am	Borrowing money from friends

---

What did he say?

He told me that ...   *He replied that ...*   *He added that ...*
He announced that ...   *He answered that ...*   *He admitted that ...*
He complained that ...   *He explained that ...*   *He suggested that ...*

Use the reporting verbs above to report the conversation on the next page.

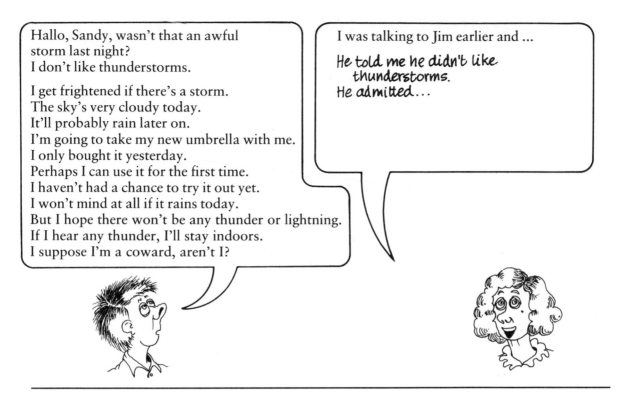

Hallo, Sandy, wasn't that an awful storm last night?
I don't like thunderstorms.

I get frightened if there's a storm.
The sky's very cloudy today.
It'll probably rain later on.
I'm going to take my new umbrella with me.
I only bought it yesterday.
Perhaps I can use it for the first time.
I haven't had a chance to try it out yet.
I won't mind at all if it rains today.
But I hope there won't be any thunder or lightning.
If I hear any thunder, I'll stay indoors.
I suppose I'm a coward, aren't I?

I was talking to Jim earlier and ...
He told me he didn't like thunderstorms.
He admitted...

Guess what!

Work in pairs. One of you should look at activity 34, while the other looks at 51. You're going to be telling your partner about a conversation you had the other day.

In other words

Transform the dialogue below into reported speech.

Annie: You really must do something about your hair, Bert.
Bert: But I like having long hair – it suits me.
Annie: Well, I think it looks ridiculous like that.
Bert: No it doesn't, it looks very.. er..very attractive.
Annie: Huh! Long hair hasn't been in fashion for years, not for men.
Bert: I don't care about fashion. What matters is whether I look nice or not.
Annie: Well, quite frankly, you don't. You look awful, especially now that you're starting to go bald.
Bert: Look, I am not going bald! I just haven't got as much hair as I used to.
Annie: You're just afraid to go to a hairdresser's in case they laugh.
Bert: Well, it's true I haven't been to a hairdresser's for ages, but...
Annie: I've got a good idea! I'll cut it for you myself. Sit down here.
Bert: I don't trust you. You'll cut it so short that people will think I've just come out of the army!

20 REPORTED SPEECH: Questions and requests

What did he want to know?

He asked (me) if ...   *He tried to find out if ...*
He wondered if ...   *He inquired if ...*
He wanted to know if ...

Imagine that you decided to pay a surprise visit on some friends last week.
Report the questions that your host asked you, using the phrases shown above.

Hallo there! Welcome!
Did you have a good journey?
When did you arrive?
Are you all right?
Have you had lunch yet?
Do you want a drink?
Did you manage to find your way easily?
Why didn't you phone us?
How long are you going to stay?
Will you be seeing anyone else while
    you're here?
Have you met my mum, who's staying too?
Do you mind sleeping on an airbed?
Why didn't you bring your sleeping bag?

He welcomed me.
He wondered if I'd had a good journey.
He asked me when I'd arrived.
He wanted ...

A very good day

1   Think for a few moments about the places you've been to and the things you've
    done in the past few weeks. Which day stands out as particularly enjoyable
    or memorable? Try to remember what happened on that very good day.

2   Work in pairs. Find out about your partner's very good day. Ask him or her:
    What happened; where he or she went to; what made it a good day; what
    might have made it even more enjoyable; how that day was different from the
    other more 'normal' days.

3   Write a report of your partner's day in just one or two paragraphs. Begin like this:
    'My partner told me ...'

What did she want you to do?

She asked me to... *She advised me to...* *She warned me (not) to...*
She told me to... *She persuaded me to...* *She invited me to...*
She wanted me to... *She encouraged me to...* *She recommended me to...*
She ordered me to... *She reminded me to...*

Use the reporting verbs above to report the conversation. Can you show what
the function of each sentence might be too?

	Function	*Report*

Please stop following me around and go away.	ORDER	She told me to stop following her around and go away.
I wonder if you'd mind opening the door.	REQUEST	She asked me to...
If I were you I'd wear a raincoat.	ADVICE	
You'd enjoy spending a weekend at our place.		
I hope you can manage dinner with us tonight.		
And don't forget to bring a bottle of wine.		
You won't regret visiting my country.		
Go on, you may win if you enter the contest!		
Don't go too near the edge of the lake.		
Get out of here and don't come back!		
Could you give me a hand please?		
It's best to learn these words by heart.		

In other words

1 Work in large groups. Half of each group should look at activity 31 while the
   other half look at activity 48. You'll see there two different versions of the
   same conversation, which you'll have to rewrite in dialogue form.
2 When you have finished rewriting the conversations, join the other half of
   your group again and show your version to your partners. What seem to be
   the differences? What was *really* said, do you think?

21 PREPOSITIONAL PHRASES I

IN

in bed, hospital, prison, jail, church
pencil, ink, pen, ballpoint
the snow, the rain, the sun, the cold, the wet, the fog
a red hat, a green cardigan, a dirty raincoat, his slippers
the evening, the night, the daytime, the morning, the afternoon
private, public, silence, secret
a loud voice, a soft voice, a whisper, a squeaky voice, a deep voice,
    a kind voice
a bad temper, a good mood, a foul mood, good spirits
danger, trouble, difficulties, love, pain, tears, debt, a hurry
sight, pieces, reach, store, flames, turn, stock, luck, the end

Complete each sentence in at least *two* ways, using the phrases above:

Everyone laughed when he came to school ....

I'd rather be .... than ....

It's boring here indoors – let's go out ....

I usually read the newspaper ....

Poor Sam! He's got to spend three weeks ....

She smiled sympathetically and then spoke to me ....

He's having a bad time and he's often ....

You can see from her expression that she's ....

Such an important meeting should be held ....

In an exam it's best to write your answers ....

Going ...

for *a walk, a drive, a ride, a run, a swim*

on *a journey, an excursion, a trip, a cruise*

by *car, bus, train, air, plane, road, sea, ship, bike*

on *a train, a ship, a bus, a bike, a plane, a ferry, a tram*
   the train, the bus, the ferry, the tram
   foot

in *a bus, a car, a train, a lift, an elevator*
   the bus, the car, the train, the lift, the elevator

Use the phrases opposite to answer these questions:

How exactly did you get to school today?
What did you do last weekend?
What did you do when you last went on holiday?
How exactly would you go from the place you're sitting now to the very
   top of the Empire State Building in New York?
What's your favourite way of travelling? Why do you prefer it?

By heart

by		on		at		out of	
	heart		*holiday*		*home*		*date*
	accident		*purpose*		*school*		*sight*
	mistake		*business*		*work*		*doors*
	day		*duty*		*university*		*danger*
	night		*strike*		*the cinema*		*work*
	myself		*my own*		*a profit*		*the question*
	itself		*fire*		*a loss*		*control*
	the way		*sale*		*hand*		*reach*
	all means		*the telephone*		*sea*		*stock*
	telephone		*the radio*		*last*		*order*
	letter		*television*		*least*		*luck*
			a diet		*the end*		*breath*

off *duty*   up to *date*   under *control*

Use the phrases in the lists above to complete each of the following sentences in
an interesting or amusing way:

I've dialled 999 because...
We can't go to London today because...
The news must be true because...
I'm sure she's very clever because...
I refuse to do any work at all because...
You can't punish them because...
They wouldn't let him enter the country because...
Go away and don't be a nuisance and...
I'm not supposed to eat chocolate because...
The only way to remember these phrases is...

Finally...

Look back through the phrases in this unit and write the *ten* phrases you find hardest to
remember in your notebook. Then compose a sentence using each phrase.

22 PREPOSITIONAL PHRASES II

Time flies!

They arrived

on **time**
in **time**
in good **time**
just in **time**
in the nick of **time**
at the same **time**

That was before my **time**
You're behind the **times**
out of **time**
He feels tired at **times**
from **time** *to time*
all the **time**
It's about **time** *you went!*
It was done in no **time** *at all*

Use the phrases above to complete each of these sentences in your own words:

If you go by plane...   Poor old Grandma, she's...
The twins...   After all this bad weather...
The lifeboat...   At the end of the exam...
Everyone ought to...   If you're going to an interview...

in time for...

in addition to   with the help of   in the mood for
in answer to   in honour of   on the point of
on behalf of   in the hope of   in search of
in charge of   by the light of   at peace with
in comparison with   in love with   at war with
in control of   by means of   in sympathy with
at the end of   in memory of   in time for

Choose one of the above phrases to complete each sentence below:

I know it's late but am I still .... dinner?
The assistant manager signed the report .... Mr Brown.
Mr Brown is the person who is .... this department.
My sister says that she's .... her maths teacher!
We're having a big party .... Mum and Dad's golden wedding.
I was .... leaving when you arrived.
The audience started clapping and cheering .... the show.
I could see a figure hiding in the cellar .... my torch.
They're playing Beatles records on the radio .... John Lennon.
I think I'll go out for a walk because I'm not .... studying.
The magician lifted the table .... his two assistants.
The two countries are still .... each other after all this time.
.... your question, wait and see!
They went up the Amazon in 1925 .... Eldorado.

44

On the one hand...

on the one hand ... on the other hand
in other words
in fact/as a matter of fact
in any case/at any rate
in theory
according to him/in his opinion

for example/for instance
in general
on the whole
in the long run
in practice

The phrases above can be used in these sentences to show the logical connection between the parts of each sentence.

There are two ways of looking at this issue: .... our profits will probably
  rise, but .... we'll have to make some sacrifices.
I'm going to have to take $500 as pocket money, ... that's what I was told.
Jack has some strange ideas: ....women are inferior to men!
I see what you mean and .... I agree with you but I don't think your
  ideas will work ....
There are a number of changes to be made: ....staff must arrive on time
  in the morning.
He isn't the best of my students: .... he ought to work much harder.
I know it's not a pleasant thing to have to do, but I'm sure that .... you
  won't regret doing it.

A little walk

Fill the gaps in this story with *one or more* words, using the phrases you have
learnt in this unit and the previous one.

The weather was so nice .... the afternoon that I decided to go
.... a little walk .... my new boots – the ones I'd seen
advertised .... TV as 'the world's best boots'. Well, ...
theory, yes, they were very comfortable boots but I soon found that
.... fact they gave me blisters. Now, ... I do enjoy walking
but by now I was .... such a lot of pain that I was .... a very
bad mood. All I wanted was rest and refreshment, ... I
needed to sit down, have a drink and go home .... the bus. The last
bus home was in half an hour from the nearest village so I would have to get
there .... a hurry. .... last I got to the village ....
time for a drink at the pub before the bus came. I limped to the bus stop
.... the hope .... getting on, but I was .... luck
because the bus was full up – not even standing room! I knew I'd never make it
home .... foot and I was .... the point ....
returning to the pub to drown my sorrows when another bus came round the
corner, completely empty. I got on, bought my ticket, sat .... at the
back and started to feel .... peace .... the world again as I
took off my boots!

23 ARTICLES: *a, the* or *Ø*?

Apples

Lady: Would you like .... apple?
Guest: Ooh, yes please! I love .... apples.
Lady: Well, there's .... big one and ....
small ones.
Guest: Oh, I'll have .... small one please.
Lady: Are you sure you won't have .... big one?
Guest: Yes, thanks. Mmm! What .... tasty apple!
Lady: Good. And I'll have .... big one myself.

1 Work in pairs and act out similar conversations about some other fruit:
   bananas, oranges, peaches, pears, apricots, plums, figs, dates, etc.
2 Make general statements about your likes and dislikes of the things to eat
   listed below. Use sentences like these:
   I normally like apples because ... but the apple I had yesterday was ...
   Usually I think bananas are horrible because ... but the banana I tried just now was ...
   As a rule I love tea because ... but the tea they serve here is ...

apples	olives	sandwiches	eggs	toast	chocolate
lemons	raisins	biscuits	tea	jam	fish
pineapples	cakes	hamburgers	coffee	butter	steaks

What a job!

Would you rather be a child or an adult?
I think I'd rather be a child.
Why?
Because children don't have to worry about...

1 Work in pairs and follow the same pattern to talk about these people. Give
   your reasons for your preferences.

doctor	patient	officer	soldier
teacher	student	referee	player
driver	passenger	millionaire	poor person
customer	shop assistant	criminal	policeman
employer	employee	actor	member of the audience

2 What jobs or professions do you think these students are going to take up
   when they finish their studies?

Alex: theology   Eddie: cookery   Ian: typing
Brian: medicine   Fiona: pharmacy   Jane: law
Carol: sociology   Geoff: modern languages
Diana: history   Hilary: creative writing

I'M STUDYING THEOLOGY

ARE YOU GOING TO BE A PRIEST? OR A TEACHER PERHAPS

In bed

Fill in the gaps below with *a* or *an* or *the* or *Ø*.

If you've got a cold, do you go to .... bed or go to .... work as usual?

Do you buy your clothes at .... local shop or in .... town?

If you wanted to learn Russian, would you go to .... school or use .... dictionary?

Do you usually eat a lot for .... lunch or do you just have .... snack?

When you look out of .... window in .... room you're in now, what can you see?

What kind of .... music do you like: .... jazz, ... rock or .... classical music?

Do you know someone who has been to ....United States, ... North Africa or .... Soviet Union?

Do you come to .... school by .... car, on .... foot or on .... bus?

Spot the errors

Each of the sentences below has two errors in it. Work in pairs and correct the mistakes you find.

```
I love a mountains and I adore a seaside too.

I've got the headache and I need a aspirin.

I don't like talking on a telephone, I prefer to write the letters.

He's the very good friend of mine even though he has the bad temper.

He's studying the music because he wants to become famous musician.

I'm going to watch a TV tonight to see a film about the Cambridge University.

I read in newspaper that we're going to have a fine weather.

When a police arrived, they questioned all people in the building.
```

A writer's life

Fill in this passage with *a* or *an* or *the* or *some* or *Ø*.

As .... writer, I seem to spend .... most of .... time working at .... home in .... office, sitting in .... front of .... typewriter. In fact, ... only people I see regularly are .... members of my family and it is difficult to keep in .... touch with .... friends I made at .... school. I'm always getting .... letters and .... phone calls from .... people at .... publisher's, though, and I do try to go out of .... house at least once .... day. And from .... time to time I give lectures or take part in .... courses at .... conferences or at .... schools in .... UK or .... abroad and this helps to prevent me feeling too isolated. I also get .... reports back from .... schools where .... material I've written is being tried out, and this kind of .... feedback is very useful. Still, it seems to me that while I'm still busy and continue to make .... living, I should go on writing .... books. But as soon as .... ideas seem to be drying up or I start suffering from .... loneliness, I'll give up .... writing and get back into .... classroom and meet .... students again.

24 *If* SENTENCES: Types 1 and 2

If and *unless*

TAKE THESE TABLETS IF YOU'RE IN PAIN, BUT DON'T TAKE THEM UNLESS YOU NEED THEM. TAKE ONE EVERY HOUR TILL THE PAIN GOES AWAY.

Use *if*, *unless*, *when*, *till* or *until* in these sentences. In some cases there are several possibilities.

It won't work .... you put batteries in.
Come and see me .... you feel lonely.
Don't phone me .... you need my help.
You can't do it .... you have permission.

Let's wait .... our friends arrive.
Let's have coffee .... we've finished.
We'll drive .... you want to walk.
I can't work .... you keep interrupting.

What are you going to do?

Imagine that you have various plans for spending the day tomorrow, depending on the weather and other circumstances. Follow the pattern below to talk about your intentions.

I might go for a walk if the weather's fine.

And what if it isn't fine?

Well, I'm certainly not going for a walk unless the weather *is* fine!

ACTIVITY	DEPENDS ON
walk	weather being fine
shopping	having enough money
theatre	getting tickets
zoo	friends being keen
swimming	weather being warm
dinner	finding good restaurant
cinema	good film being on
work	being in the mood

If, if, if...

IF I PASS THE EXAM, I'LL BUY EVERYONE A DRINK

IF I KNEW MORE, I'D BE SURE TO PASS

IF I HADN'T WASTED SO MUCH TIME, I'D HAVE LEARNT MORE

Fill the gaps in these sentences with the correct verb forms:

If you drive carefully, you .... have any accidents.
If I .... a better driver, I .... have so many accidents.
If I .... carefully last night, I .... an accident.
If I .... President of the United States, I ....

Just suppose...

How would you feel?
How would your life be different... **if you were much...**

> *younger   taller   more intelligent   more patient*
> *older   shorter   less intelligent   less patient*   than you really are?

Or if you were:
> *famous   blind   deaf   very poor   very good-looking?*

Work in small groups and encourage each other to answer the questions.

First prize!

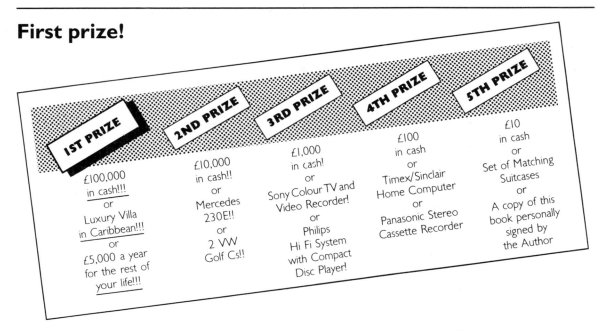

Imagine that you have entered this competition and are dreaming about the various prizes you might win. Which prizes would you choose to have instead of taking the money? If you took the cash, what would you spend it on?

Complete the sentences

If I get up late tomorrow, ...
If it snows a lot this winter, ...
If I lived in the USA, ...
If I have a headache tomorrow, ...
If I were a nicer person, ...
Unless you leave immediately, ...

I won't come and see you if ...
I wouldn't be very happy if ...
The world would be a better place if ...
I'm not going out tonight unless ...
I would speak perfect English if ...
I'll take a message if ...

25 *If* SENTENCES: Type 3

She didn't win

Poor Mary! She was sure she was going to
win, but she didn't. What could she have
done if she had won, do you think?
Write down five sentences beginning:

'If Mary had won ...'

If I'd been there...

Work in pairs. Imagine what you might have seen or could have done if you'd
been in the following places at the right time. Look at the example first:

IF I'D BEEN IN BELGIUM IN 1815, I MIGHT
HAVE SEEN NAPOLEON DEFEATED AT WATERLOO.

1966	Last live Beatles concert in San Francisco
1969	Apollo XI took off from Cape Kennedy for the Moon
1976	First commercial Concorde flights (Paris–Rio and London–Bahrain)
1976	Winter Olympics in Innsbruck, Austria
1978–9	Revolution in Iran
1980	Bjorn Borg's 5th Wimbledon title
1981	Prince Charles's marriage to Lady Diana Spencer
1982	World Cup Finals in Madrid
1983	Pope John Paul's visit to Poland
1984	Olympic Games in Los Angeles

Luckily...

Complete each sentence with your own ideas.

Luckily my brakes worked all right, *but if* ...
  I soon got better, but if ...
  I only got a black eye, but if ...
  I got the job easily enough, but if ...
  the rain stopped after breakfast, but if ...
  I got to the cinema early enough, but if ...
  our pilot managed to land the plane on one engine, but if ...

Just imagine...!

1 Just imagine if you'd been born a member of the opposite sex...
   what would have happened to you?
   what wouldn't have happened to you that has actually
       happened in reality?
   how would your life have been different so far?
   and how would your life be different now?

2 And just imagine if you'd been born in the United States...
   If you'd been born the son or daughter of a millionaire...
   If you'd been born with an ability to see the future...
   If you'd been born a genius...

Work in small groups and encourage each other to be as imaginative as
possible!

In other words

We stayed up all night and that's why we're all so tired this morning.
We...

She wasn't able to answer the questions and so she failed the exam.
If she...

I didn't see you there, otherwise I'd have said hallo.
If I...

The reason why I haven't been to America is that I can't afford it.
If I...

He hasn't studied English before and that's why he's in a beginners class.
If he...

They didn't go to the seaside because the weather was so bad.
They...

One of the reasons why I didn't phone you was that I was very busy.
I might...

They won the match because two of our players were injured.
If...

Three paragraphs

Write three paragraphs, beginning as follows:
   'If the weather's nice this weekend...'
   'If I had lots of money...'
   'If I'd worked harder at school...'

26 RELATIVE CLAUSES

This is the man who...

How do you think this conversation might continue?

THIS IS THE MAN WHO HAS ASKED ME TO MARRY HIM

GOOD GRIEF! THAT'S THE MAN I WAS TELLING YOU ABOUT !!

What's she called?

Work in pairs. One of you should look at activity 35 and the other at 44. Talk about the girls in the cartoon, following this pattern.

A: What's the girl who's wearing glasses called?
   or What's the name of the girl who's wearing glasses?
   or What's the name of the girl in glasses?
B: She's called Anne.
A: Oh, really? She's the girl I met in London years ago.

What's it about?

Work in groups of three. One of you should look at activity 37, another at 43 and another at 56. You're going to be telling each other what the following books, plays, films or stories are about. Use this pattern:
   'What's *Hamlet* about?'   'It's about a man who wants to kill his father's murderer.'

HAMLET   DON QUIXOTE   MOBY DICK   REMEMBRANCE OF THINGS PAST
THE GRAPES OF WRATH   SNOW WHITE   GOLDILOCKS   BABES IN THE WOOD
SUPERMAN   POPEYE   CITIZEN KANE   THE DAY OF THE JACKAL
JAWS   E.T.   TOM AND JERRY   DALLAS   KING KONG   KING LEAR

My friend John, whose ...

Use *where*, *when*, *who*, *that* or *which* to complete each sentence. Be very careful about where you put the commas!

The place ....*where I went to*........... school   is a delightful town.
Edinburgh**,** .... college**,** is a beautiful city.
My eldest brother   .... moustache   is studying architecture.
The man   .... television   is a famous writer.
The day   .... married   was Friday the 13th.
On Wednesday   .... cinema   it rained all day.
The car   ....stolen   was a yellow Rolls Royce.
My car   1965   is a yellow Morris 1000.
Liverpool   .... First Division   have an unbeatable team.
But the team   ....Cup Final   are in the Second Division.

Connections

Use *who* or *which* to make single sentences, as in the example below:
   I saw Peter. He saw me. He waved at me.
   I saw Peter, who waved at me when he saw me.

Mary ate four cream cakes. This made her feel sick.
I'm going on holiday to the mountains. I'm really looking forward to this.
I went to see a film. It was about space monsters. It gave me nightmares.
We started talking to Bernard. He told us about his adventures in the jungle.
I wrote them an angry letter. This made me feel much calmer afterwards.
I spent a long time with James. He was very helpful. He gave me some good advice.
You'd better rewrite this letter. You wrote it far too quickly and carelessly.

In other words

He was wearing old and dirty clothes.   The clothes ...
I started work on January 2nd.   The day ...
I was given the message by someone wearing a yellow pullover.   The person ...
My favourite film is 'Some Like it Hot', made in 1959.   'Some Like it Hot' ...
An old school friend gave me a kiss.   The girl ...
You were rude to that lady's husband and she's upset now.   The lady ...
I bought a new pair of shoes in the sale.   The shoes ...
I love the colour green – it reminds me of the countryside.   Green ...

27 ADJECTIVES AND VERBS + PREPOSITION I

Any good at maths?

1 Work in pairs and note down the names of five outdoor sports, five indoor games and five subjects you studied at school.

2 Join another pair and find out how good they are or were at the games and subjects on your list.

brilliant	*quite good*	*pretty bad*
superb	*not bad*	*no good*
very good	*so-so*	*hopeless*
pretty good	*not very good*	*terrible*

NO, BUT I USED TO BE QUITE GOOD AT HISTORY

How do you feel?

She's ...
getting the job.

He's ...
tomorrow's exam.

She's ...
going out alone at night.

He's ...
being kept waiting.

She's ...
missing the show.

He's ...
leaving his girlfriend.

1 Which of these phrases go with the cartoons above?

angry	*heart-broken*	*glad*	+ about	*afraid*	+ of
annoyed	*worried*	*nervous*		*scared*	
delighted	*upset*	*pleased*		*terrified*	
disappointed	*depressed*	*thrilled*		*frightened*	
happy	*furious*	*anxious*			
		sad			

2 What kind of things do *you* feel angry about, worried about, afraid of, etc.? Tell your partner.

Add the prepositions

Put a suitable preposition after each adjective and complete the sentences with your own ideas. Look at the example first.

She felt very ashamed *of slapping him on the face*...
Miss Green's a very nice lady and tries to be friendly ...
Pete's the sort of nasty person who is unkind ...
I always try to be as polite as possible ...
When Tom got promotion he was very proud ...
Life in my country is quite different ...
The insurance company wants to know who was responsible ...
Foreigners who visit my country are always impressed ...
When Mary started tennis lessons, John became very jealous ...
The little boy said he was very sorry ...
When Vera introduced Neil to her family, he was very rude ...

Rearrange the sentences

Rearrange the beginnings and ends of these sentences so that they all make good sense *and* add the missing prepositions in the middle.

Everyone praised him **for**	his own stupidity.
This house reminds me	Winston Churchill.
We congratulated him	telling lies and cheating in the exam.
I can't forgive him	doing so well in the exam.
He tried to blame us	his performance in the concert.
They named their son	a place I used to know.
He punished his son	speaking to me in such an insulting way.

Verbs + prepositions

Put a suitable preposition after the verb in each sentence and then use your own ideas to complete the sentences.

I'm excited because I'm going to take part *in this year's tennis tournament.*
I broke her glasses and she made me pay ...
He wasn't paying attention and crashed ...
I've got to stay at home tonight and prepare ...
All the furniture in this room belongs ...
Whether or not we go out depends ...
There was so much noise that I couldn't concentrate ...
The United Kingdom consists ...
It was an awful hotel and we complained ...
She made a tremendous effort and succeeded ...
We only had one cake, so it was divided ...

28 ADJECTIVES AND VERBS + PREPOSITION II

Who to? Where from?

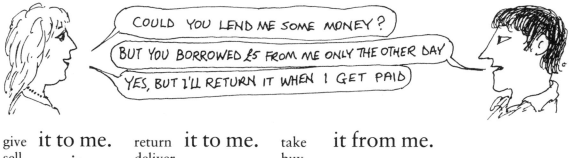

give	it to me.	return	it to me.	take	it from me.
sell	me it.	deliver		buy	
lend				borrow	
offer				get	
				steal	
				receive	

Work in pairs. Use each of the verbs above in a sentence, as in these examples:
> *They delivered the parcels to my flat.*
> *The salesman offered his customers a discount.*

or *He offered a discount to his customers.*

Add the prepositions

Find the right prepositions to fill the gaps.

I've looked everywhere .... my keys.

We searched high and low .... them.

Who's going to look .... the children while you're away?

He tends to feel embarrassed when people look .... him.

Don't you know it's rude to stare .... people?

He threw the ball .... his friend who caught it easily.

The rioters started throwing stones .... the police.

The police opened fire .... the crowd.

They went on shooting .... them until they ran away.

She gets very upset if someone shouts .... her.

Don't laugh .... him or he'll get very angry.

Afterwards they were able to laugh .... the incident.

Take no notice .... him, he's just showing off

Please pay attention .... what I tell you.

He's very tactless and doesn't care .... other people.

None for me, thanks, I don't really care .... chocolate.

Who's going to take care .... me if I feel ill?

I'd like a word ....you .... your work.

He spoke .... me ....his plans.

I disagreed .... him .... what he should do.

She talked .... him ....the book she'd read.

He argued .... her .... the opinion she'd expressed.

I had a nightmare .... prehistoric monsters.

I was dreaming .... my childhood before I woke up.

I'm dreaming .... going to Africa one day.

She's thinking .... changing her job.

I was just thinking .... how to solve the problem.

I could do .... a nice cool drink.

I can't do .... eight hours sleep a night.

I'll call .... you at 7.30 in my car.

They called him Michael .... his grandfather.

We called .... the bill after our meal.

Do you remember?

Use the phrases you have come across in this unit and in unit 27 to fill the gaps below:

He's very arrogant and gets annoyed if people ..... *disagree with* .... him.
It's all my fault – can you ever .... what I've done?
Getting the job .... how well you do at the interview.
.... passing your exams!
I'd like to .... the manager about this, please.
When I finish my studies, I'm .... travelling round the world.
I usually feel .... going anywhere by plane.
Don't be silly! There's no need to be .... flying!
I'm ever so hungry – I .... a sandwich or something.
I used to be .... spelling but now I'm a bit better.
All right, then! Which one of you .... breaking the window?
It's your own fault! Don't .... your own mistakes!
Tom's grandmother .... when his parents died.
That's a nice watch, where did you ....?
Shh! I'm trying to .... my homework.
She looks very .... something – she's actually smiling!

29 THE PASSIVE

In other words

Rewrite each sentence so that it means the same as the sentence on the left.

Someone has killed Lord Wessex.   Lord Wessex *has been killed.*
Someone found the body in the study.   The body...
The murderer committed the murder at around midnight.   The murder...
The butler saw two strangers near the house.   Two strangers...
The police are questioning the butler.   The butler...
They know that Lady Wessex was out of the country.   Lady Wessex...
No one has seen the younger son for three weeks.   The younger son...
The family last saw the elder son two years ago.   The elder son...
Everyone will sadly miss Lord Wessex.   Lord Wessex...

Who by?

The names in the second column below have all been printed in the wrong order. Can you rearrange them and make a sentence for each, giving the correct information? Look at the example on the right first.

Nicholas Nickleby   Picasso
Guernica   Charles Dickens
The Magic Flute   The Beatles
Star Wars   Schubert
The 'Unfinished' Symphony   George Lucas
Snoopy   Thomas Edison
Sergeant Pepper's Lonely
  Hearts Club Band   Alexander Fleming
Penicillin   Sony
Light bulbs   Mozart
Walkman stereo   Charles Schulz
War and Peace   Walt Disney
Mickey Mouse   Cambridge University Press
This book   Leo Tolstoy

I THINK PENICILLIN WAS DISCOVERED BY ALEXANDER FLEMING.

News headlines

Rewrite these newspaper headlines as complete sentences. Look at the example first.

Theft of valuable painting from National Gallery

A valuable painting has been stolen from the National Gallery.

Over 100 road deaths last month	*Bank manager still held by police*
24,000 murders in USA last year	**Top job for Jones in Cabinet**
Ancient statue found in garden shed	*No change in divorce law till 1994*
15 students arrested after demo	**15 new hospitals last year**
Pay rise for teachers this year	*Briton wins tennis title*

Being ...

Work in pairs for this exercise. One of you should look at activity 29, while the other looks at 49. Use the expressions below to react to each other's promises, threats and offers.

Oh dear!	*I don't like being criticised.*
How awful!	*I hate...*
Oh no!	*I can't stand...*
Being criticised is awful.	
	... is horrible.
	... isn't very nice.
I don't want to be criticised.	
I wouldn't like to...	
It's awful to...	

Great!	*I like...*
Fine!	*I love...*
Lovely!	*I enjoy...*
Being...	*... is nice.*
	... is lovely.
	... is fun.
I'd like to be...	
It's nice to...	
It's lovely to...	

Passive → Active → Passive

Rewrite each sentence. Look at the examples carefully first.

Jimmy got punished by his father.
Jimmy's father punished him.
The plants got damaged by the cold weather.
His leg was broken in a skiing accident.
Dozens of trees got blown down in the wind.
She was awarded the prize by the judges.
He got thrown out of class for cheating.
The party of tourists were shown the sights.

Someone has stolen my watch.
My watch has been stolen.
The voters re-elected the President.
The police are interviewing all the witnesses.
We're going to give him a big surprise!
The chambermaid hasn't cleaned my room.
My secretary will tell you the results.
Father Christmas gave me a video recorder.

30 WORD FORMATION: Adjectives and adverbs

Forming adjectives

1 Look at the adjectives listed below.

-y	-able	-al	-ive
cloudy	adorable	chemical	active
dusty	avoidable	habitual	attractive
funny	bearable	musical	destructive
grassy	believable	national	explosive
hairy	breakable	optional	imaginative
moody	comfortable	philosophical	offensive
sandy	enjoyable	political	progressive
sleepy	profitable	practical	receptive
snowy	readable	professional	repetitive
woolly	reliable	psychological	

THEY'RE VERY WOOLLY AREN'T THEY?
YES, THEY'RE ADORABLE

2 What are the nouns (or verbs) that correspond with the adjectives in the lists?
For example, *adorable* corresponds with *adore*, *imaginative* with *imagine*, etc.

3 Add the correct adjectival forms of the following words to the lists above:
accept, inform, logic, persuade, region, predict, speed, wind

4 For each adjective in the list, think of at least one noun that is commonly used with it.
For example:

a woolly ..*jumper, sock*.................... and a habitual *criminal, smoker*.................

Opposites

IT'S A VERY USEFUL GADGET

IT LOOKS PRETTY USELESS TO ME

HAPPY BIRTHDAY

1 Look at the adjectives in the lists below:

-ful	-less		-ful	un-
careful	careless		helpful	unhelpful
colourful	colourless		successful	unsuccessful
useful	useless		truthful	untruthful
thoughtful	thoughtless			
meaningful	meaningless			

2 Add the correct adjectival forms of the
following words to the lists above:
harm, event, pain, power, tune

3 For each adjective in the lists, think of at least one noun that is commonly used with it.
For example:

a careful .*driver*...............

Forming adverbs

Work in small groups or pairs. Complete each sentence, using any suitable adverbs apart from *well* or *badly*. Look at the example first:

A good driver *drives slowly.*   A bad driver *drives carelessly.*
A good student...   A bad student...
A good friend...   An enemy...
A good teacher...   A bad teacher...
A good person...   A wicked person...

What's he or she like?

Use the adjectives and adverbs from the rest of the unit to describe:
    five people in the room around you, and
    five members of your family.
You may also find it useful to look at the list below of adjectives like *oldish*
(= 'sort of old' or 'fairly old'):

youngish   oldish
tallish   shortish
greyish   straightish
reddish

Fill in the gaps

Sheep are .... creatures.

Careful – that antique bowl is .... !

Dr Jekyll drank the .... liquid.

Prof. White has .... hair.

The President is a .... man.

I find electronic music very ....

She is a .... nail-biter.

I found the story very ....

I'm afraid they write rather ....

I hope you're .... in the exam.

31 WORD FORMATION: Verbs

Make it tighter!

1 Use one of the verbs below to complete the sentences on the right.

to *tighten   sharpen*   I didn't mean to .... you. Sorry.
   loosen   shorten   This dress needs to be ....
   flatten   soften   Could someone .... this knife for me?
   frighten   sweeten   The building was .... by the explosion.
   harden   thicken   The sauce tastes nice but it needs to be ....
   weaken

2 Do the same with the next set of sentences after you have studied the list
below. Careful: if there are several possibilities, choose the one you think is the best.

to *cool   lower*   The food's ready, it only needs ....
   clean   lift   They used steel bars to .... the wall.
   dry   raise   I really ought to .... my shoes.
   enlarge   purify   Use these tablets to .... the water.
   heat   simplify   I can't .... this sofa all by myself.
   warm   strengthen   After the ceremony the flag was ....
              The text has been .... for foreign students.

Do it again!

Use one of the verbs below to complete the sentences on the right.

to *redo*

rebuild   reassemble   I'd like you to .... this letter.
reconsider   retype   It's high time my flat was ....
reprint   replant   He took the radio to pieces but then
remarry   rewrite   he couldn't .... it.
refurnish   rethink   We were all surprised when she ....
refreeze   redecorate   at the age of 85.
refloat   repaint   A Christmas tree can sometimes be ....
              in your garden.
              The book's so popular that it's been ....
              six times.

Use your imagination...

How many things can you think of which you can...		And what may happen if you ...
unbutton	or button up?	overeat?
untie	or tie up	overwork
unfold	or fold up	oversleep
unscrew	or screw up	overcook something
undo	or do up	overload something
uncover	or cover up	are overcharged?
unroll	or roll up	
unzip	or zip up?	

Did you understand correctly?

Use the verbs below to complete the sentences on the right.

misbehave   It doesn't normally matter if you .... a word in English.

miscalculate   He crashed because he .... the other car's speed.

misinform   As usual, the children have been ....

misjudge   No, I'm not resigning. You must have been ....

misread   I'm sorry, I think I .... the instructions you gave us.

mispronounce   She missed the train because she .... the timetable.

misunderstand   They .... the amount of money they had spent.

Complete the sentences

The words in capitals at the end of each sentence can be used to form a word that fits suitably in the blank space. Look at the example first.

Sorry I'm late, my alarm clock didn't go off and I _overslept._	SLEEP
Vegetables taken from the freezer should not be	FREEZE
The palace was burnt down in the war and later it was	BUILD
The dam burst because it had been .... by the earthquake.	WEAK
I can't .... the lid of this jar of jam.	SCREW
Excuse me, waiter, I think you've .... us for the wine.	CHARGE
If you continue .... you may end up in hospital.	WORK
The committee was asked to .... its decision.	CONSIDER
The ship was firmly stuck on the rocks and couldn't be	FLOAT
I'm afraid there has been a slight	UNDERSTAND

32 WORD FORMATION: Abstract nouns

Adjectives → nouns

1 Fill the gaps in the chart below with the appropriate forms. Find out the
meanings of any words you don't understand. Be careful about spelling!

-ness

happy	happiness
clever	*cleverness*
mean	*meanness*
shy	
kind	
polite	
cold	coldness
	selfishness
neat	
tidy	
nervous	

-ity

stupid	stupidity
popular	*popularity*
original	
possible	
responsible	
equal	
	certainty
	reliability
	inferiority
superior	
probable	
necessary	
sincere	
mature	
pure	
rare	

-ence

violent	violence
patient	
	confidence
intelligent	

2 Now do the same with these more difficult examples. Use a dictionary or ask
a partner if you have any difficulties.

proud	pride	efficient	efficiency	friend	friendship
hungry			warmth	leader	
anxious		hot		accurate	accuracy
safe			height	loyal	
thirsty		deep		bored	
honest		long		optimistic	
sympathetic		strong			pessimism
true			width	realistic	
	wisdom		breadth	brave	
	anger				relevance

3 Use suitable abstract nouns to complete each of these sentences:
She's blushing because of her __shyness__.   Pandas are protected because of their r ....
I enjoy the r .... of my new job.   I love dogs because of their l ....
There's too much v .... on TV.   You might at least show some s .... !
The Thames is 346 km in l ....   These exercises will increase your s ....
I swear to you that I'm telling the t ....   I believe in e .... between men and women.
He suffers from n .... before an exam.   Teachers are said to need a lot of p ....

Verbs → nouns

1 Fill the gaps in the chart. Be careful with your spelling!

-ment		-ion		-ation	
announce	announcement	discuss	discussion	admire	admiration
arrange	*arrangement*	complete		organise	
develop		repeat		hesitate	
amaze		suspect		educate	
excite		oppose			information
	disappointment		destruction		qualification
embarrass			contribution		concentration
amuse			decision	vary	
treat			satisfaction	apply	
	argument		connection	pronounce	
	enjoyment	permit		explain	
	astonishment	receive		cancel	
		compare		expect	
		interrupt		form	

2 Now try these more difficult ones. Ask a partner or use a dictionary if you have any difficulties.

arrive	arrival	die	death	complain	
survive	*survival*	be born			obedience
approve		prove		break	
perform	performance		laughter		signature
disappear			loss	succeed	
assist		choose			
resist		behave			
insist	insistence		failure		
prefer		please			
persist		believe			

3 Use suitable abstract nouns to complete each of these sentences:

We were given a warm ...reception...

The pianist gave a wonderful p ....

I hope I've made the right c ....

I didn't understand the e ....

He couldn't understand my p ....

They have no p .... of his guilt.

Allow him to speak without i ....

I'd like to make a serious c ....

In c .... with him, she's a genius.

They celebrated the b .... of their 7th son.

The expedition ended in complete f ....

She asked her parents' p .... to get married.

They had no s .... that he was the thief.

Thanks for your kind a ....

To my e .... I had forgotten my wallet.

To our a .... he had forgotten the date.

The children were on their best b ....

The whole show was a great s ....

33 WORD FORMATION: Opposites

Negative forms

1 Look carefully through the words below. Make sure you understand them all:

un *able breakable comfortable conscious expected fair familiar known like likely lucky married musical necessary pleasant predictable popular real reliable reasonable related safe satisfactory tidy willing wise*

unlucky

in *accurate capable complete convenient direct efficient experienced sensitive tolerant visible*

dis *obedient satisfied*
comfort pleasure
agree approve courage like obey please prove

2 Add the negative forms of the following words to the lists above:
  advantage certain common convenient correct fit
  friendly kind grateful honest ready ripe sincere

3 Use the words from the lists above to complete these sentences:

The chair is rather ....
The result of the match was ....
My old car is rather ....
Their behaviour .... their parents.
I .... of smoking in restaurants.

They seem rather .... of foreigners.
They look alike but in fact they're ....
She is .... to pass the test.
After the accident he was ....
Eating .... fruit is bad for you.

4 Now look at these, rather more difficult, negative forms. What is the positive form of each of them?

impossible	*impractical*	*illegal*	*irregular*	*non-drip*
imperfect	*impure*	*illiterate*	*irrelevant*	*non-fiction*
impatient	*impassable*	*illogical*	*irresponsible*	*non-slip*
impersonal	*immature*	*illegible*	*irresistible*	*non-stick*
improbable	*immoral*	*illegitimate*	*irrational*	*non-smoker*

5 Use words from the lists above to complete the following sentences:

Large hotels can be very ....
The point he made seems .... to me.
The library contains mostly .... books.

He is a passionate ....
40% of the population are ....
Her signature was ....

What's the opposite of ... ?

1 Work in pairs. Write the opposite of each of the words below in the spaces provided. Use a dictionary if necessary.

happy   *sad*
warm
nice
beautiful
raw
wealthy
smooth
enormous

gentle
shy
wide
deep
fresh
absent
ill
cruel

angry
lazy
rude
asleep
foolish
noisy
arrogant
tame

sleepy
generous
modern
cheap
dangerous
cowardly
miserable
difficult

2 For each adjective above, think of one noun with which it can be used.

For example: a wild ....*animal*...., an expensive .*fur coat*........, etc.

3 Use words from the lists above to complete the following sentences:

I waited for my soup to get ....   Is it .... to cross the river?
He was too .... to lend me the money.   Yes, the river's very ....
I can't eat this bread, it's too ....   1,000 people were .... at the meeting.
I'm not tired, I'm ....   I prefer to stay in .... hotels.
The Japanese like to eat .... fish.   I had flu last week but now I'm .... again.

Complete the sentences 🖉

The words in capitals at the end of each sentence can be used to form a word that fits suitably into the blank space. Look at the example first.

The contestants protested about the judges' ..*unfairness*................................   FAIR
The audience expressed their .... by booing and whistling.   APPROVE
Marks will be deducted in the exam for grammatical ....   ACCURATE
She frowned at them to show her ....   PLEASE
The father was imprisoned for his .... to the children.   CRUEL
The dog was beaten by its owner for its ....   OBEY
I can't predict the results of the election with any ....   CERTAIN
After our .... we are no longer on speaking terms.   AGREE
We wish to apologise to passengers for any .... caused by the strike.   CONVENIENT
The children held each other tight for ....   WARM
I'm sorry about the .... of my desk.   TIDY

34 QUANTITY AND NUMBERS

How much? How many?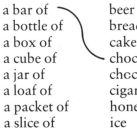

1 Rearrange the items below so that they match. The first has been done for you.

a bar of	beer		a box of	lemonade
a bottle of	bread		a can of	matches
a box of	cake		a packet of	milk
a cube of	chocolate		a pot of	paper
a jar of	chocolates		a carton of	sugar
a loaf of	cigarettes		a jug of	tea
a packet of	honey		a sheet of	toothpaste
a slice of	ice		a tube of	water

2 Now one of you should look at activity 28 while the other looks at 53.

So much! So many!

Fit both of the words in the columns on the right
into the sentences using *so much* or *so many*
correctly. Look at the example first.

They've got *so many possessions/so much money*   *possession*   *money*
    that everyone envies them.
I received ..... that I couldn't make up my mind what to do.   *advice*   *suggestion*
I had to learn ..... that I got a splitting headache.   *information*   *fact*
The professor wants to do ..... that he needs a new laboratory.   *research*   *experiments*
My friends have ..... that they'll soon need a bigger house.   *armchair*   *furniture*
We had to do ..... that we didn't finish till midnight.   *homework*   *exercise*
I had to carry ..... that my arms were aching.   *luggage*   *bag*
We've heard ..... that we know everything about it now.   *report*   *news*
This encyclopedia contains ..... that you need no other books.   *knowledge*   *reference*

And add your own endings to these sentences:

During our holiday we had ....   *sunshine*
The students in this class have made ....   *progress*
There was ....   *traffic*
In English there seem(s) to be ....   *vocabulary*

How many can you count?

Work in pairs. Count aloud the number of sides, squares and triangles in the drawings. (The answers are 35, 27, 26 and 30 – but not in that order!)

How many sides?   How many squares?   How many triangles   How many squares?

 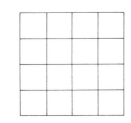 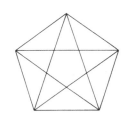 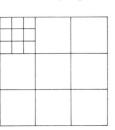

High numbers

Take it in turns with your partner to say aloud the phrases below. Look carefully at the example before you start:

1 wonderful woman 11   111   1,111   11,111   111,111   1,111,111
'one wonderful woman, eleven wonderful women,
one hundred and eleven wonderful women,
one thousand one hundred and eleven wonderful women...'

2 terrified tourists	22	222	2,222	22,222	222,222	2,222,222
3 thirsty thieves	33	333	3,333	33,333	333,333	3,333,333
4 fortunate fools	44	444	4,444	44,444	444,444	4,444,444
5 fine firemen	55	555	5,555	55,555	555,555	5,555,555
6 silly citizens	66	666	6,666	66,666	666,666	6,666,666
7 selfish secretaries	77	777	7,777	77,777	777,777	7,777,777
8 aged traitors	88	888	8,888	88,888	888,888	8,888,888
9 nice neighbours	99	999	9,999	99,999	999,999	9,999,999

Arithmetic ▨

Work in pairs. One of you should look at activity 16 and the other at 45.

Fill the gaps

Can you work out or guess the missing words or numbers in the sentences below? Do this exercise orally and not only in writing!

3 .... 37 equals 111.
If you .... 222 by 37, you get 6.
If you .... 37 by 9, the answer is 333.
37 × 12 .... 444.
37 × 15 ....
37 × 18 ....

$11^2 = 121$
$111^2 = 12,321$
$...............^2 = 1,234,321$
$11,111^2 = ..., ..., ...$
$111,111^2 = 12, ..., ..., ...$
.... $= 12,345,678,987,654,321$

69

35 JOINING SENTENCES I

When ...

I was drinking my beer when John came back.

I had drunk my beer when John came back.

I drank my beer when John came back.

Use your own words to complete each sentence in this story:

When he heard the phone ringing, ...
When he got to the phone, ...
When it rang again, ...
When he heard his fiancée's voice, ...
When she told him the news, ...

When he had got over the shock, ...
When he put down the receiver, ...
When the phone rang again later, ...
When we saw him the next morning, ...

Rearrange the sentences

Match the two halves of each sentence so that all the sentences make sense.
The first one has been done for you.

I held my breath
I didn't leave the room
I bought a new coat
I used to get into trouble
I forgot to wash my hands
I sent the parcel
I had eaten all her chocolates
I went on holiday
I waited patiently
I was able to do the exercise

until I had finished all my work.
when I'd saved up enough money.
as the door slowly opened.
by the time she came back.
till they arrived.
whenever I came home late.
soon after I heard the exam results.
before I had dinner.
as soon as I found out the address.
once I'd found the answers in the back.

Complete the sentences

Rewrite each sentence so that it still means the same. Look at the example first.

We had a meal before the programme.   ...before the programme started.
We had coffee during the programme.   ...while...
We turned the TV off after the programme.   ...after...
We discussed the programme until bedtime.   ...until...
I haven't enjoyed a film so much since Superman III.   ...since...

I had cheese on toast before I went to bed, ,before *going to bed*
I had a terrible nightmare while I was asleep. ...during ,
I couldn't sleep after I had woken up. ...after...
I stayed awake till it became light. ...till...
I haven't slept so badly since I was a child. ...since...

Fill the gaps

Find a suitable word or words to fill each gap in these sentences:

She wears a swimming cap ....*whenever*...... she goes swimming.
He'd smoked 20 cigarettes .... it was his turn to speak.
They gave us the results .... we'd been waiting for two hours.
The survivors waited 24 hours .... they were rescued.
I haven't laughed so much .... Father fell into the river.
I try to do plenty of revision .... I take an exam.
He took his coat and hat off .... he came into the house.
They waited in silence .... the policeman had gone past.
You shouldn't have called to her .... she was crossing the road.

Late for work again!

Complete each sentence in this story about someone who arrived late for work:

I couldn't leave home until *the post had come.*
I read my mail before ....
I walked to the bus stop after ....
I had to queue at the stop till ....
I read the paper while ....
I'd been waiting for half an hour by the time ....
I continued reading the paper during ....
I jumped off the bus as soon as ....
I got some dirty looks from everyone in the office when ....

Join the sentences

Make a single sentence from each of these pairs of sentences.

He has been at college for 2½ years.   During that time he seems to have learnt nothing.
I reported the theft of my passport.   Afterwards I discovered it in my suitcase.
I paid £200 for a suit.   Later I saw the same suit at half the price.
He told me he was your brother.   Until then I had no idea who he was.
I did a lot of work.   Before that I decided to take the phone off the hook.
She was terribly rude to me.   After that she tried to apologise.
She saw it was raining.   She immediately rushed into the garden to get the washing.
You're going to leave the house.   Beforehand, make sure you lock the door.
You're going to finish this exercise.   Afterwards, you can have a well-earned rest.

71

36 JOINING SENTENCES II

Just in case

in case
because, as
although, even though
so that
if, as long as, provided that
unless

I'm wearing sunglasses...
   in case the sun shines later.
   because the sun may shine.
   even though it's not sunny now.

Use the words shown above to complete the following sentences:

He's brought an umbrella ....*in case*........... it rains later.
He's wearing a hat .... he doesn't want us to know that he's bald.
He's going to bed with a hot water bottle .... it's midsummer.
The town was flooded .... it had rained so heavily.
I've brought some sandwiches .... I feel hungry.
I didn't go to bed .... I had an awful cold.
I have to wear glasses .... I can see to read.
You can teach me to drive .... you promise not to lose your temper.
I won't speak to her again .... she apologises.
I'm going dancing tonight .... my ankle's swollen.

In other words

Rewrite each sentence so that it still means the same.

We went swimming despite the rain.   Although ...
The trains were late due to bad weather.   Because the weather ...
He broke the teapot because of his clumsiness.   Because ...
They passed the test in spite of their laziness.   Even though ...
She left early so as to catch her train.   She left early so that ...
I lost my temper due to their stupid behaviour.   As ...

Both ... and ...

	ANNE	CHARLES	EDWARD	ANDREW
meat	√	√	✗	✗
fish	√	√	✗	√
rice	✗	✗	✗	√
potatoes	√	✗	√	✗
pasta	√	√	√	√
eggs	√	√	✗	√
bananas	✗	√	√	✗

Both Anne and Charles like meat.
Neither Edward nor Andrew likes meat.

Edward dislikes both meat and fish.
Edward doesn't like either meat or fish.
Edward likes neither meat nor fish.

Only Andrew likes rice.
None of them likes rice except Andrew.
Everyone except Andrew dislikes rice.

1 Make up more similar sentences about the people in the chart.
2 Devise a similar chart and find out about the likes and dislikes of the people in your group.
3 Write sentences about the people in your group, trying to use a number of different structures as in the sentences on the previous page.

Uncles

Work in pairs. One of you should look at activity 23 while the other looks at 54.
You're going to describe and draw some uncles!

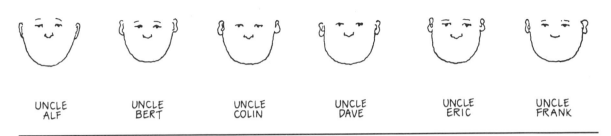

UNCLE ALF UNCLE BERT UNCLE COLIN UNCLE DAVE UNCLE ERIC UNCLE FRANK

And, but...

Use the word on the right of each sentence to make a sentence that means the same. Look at the example first.

John likes dancing and Mary likes dancing.   both
Both John and Mary like dancing.

He felt depressed and rang up his friend.   because
It's past my bedtime but I'm going to stay up.   although
Do that again and you'll get into trouble.   if
My father doesn't smoke and my mother doesn't either.   neither
I'm feeling ill but I'm going to work anyway.   even though
You'd better go to bed or you won't get better.   unless
I adore oranges and I think grapefruit are delicious.   both

Rewrite the sentences

Join up these pairs of sentences to make single longer sentences.

There was fog at the airport. This had caused all flights to be delayed.
All flights were delayed because of fog at the airport.

Ann and Tim were waiting for the same flight. As a result they started talking.
She was feeling very hungry. The reason was that she hadn't had breakfast.
He offered her a sandwich. Being so hungry she accepted the offer.
They had a common interest in music. That was why they got on well.
He adored playing the piano. And so did she.
She was much older than him. Nevertheless he found her very attractive.
They had a big row next day. Still, they decided to get married.
He enjoyed her cooking. Furthermore he enjoyed her company too.
He never let her go out alone. This was to prevent her meeting any other men.

37 JOINING SENTENCES III: Links between sentences

Time adverbs

Before that   Earlier
After that   Afterwards   Later
Meanwhile   At the same time

Use the adverbs above to connect the pairs of sentences. Look at the example first.

The hostage struggled to get free. ....*Meanwhile*.... the robbers were sharing out the money.
He ate two dozen oysters. .... he had a terrible stomachache.
I'm going off to play a round of golf. .... I'd like you to get on with the work.
They spent the night on the mountain. .... I'd warned them not to go up there.
We assumed a burglar had broken the window. .... we found nothing was missing.
I waited and waited for her to arrive. .... she was stuck in the lift.
The washing got soaked in the rain. .... the sun came out and dried it all.
Over 30 people came to the party. .... we'd only bought enough food for about 10.

Reason, contrast, result

That's why   Therefore
Nevertheless   Nonetheless
Otherwise
Alternatively   On the other hand
However

Use the adverbs above to connect these pairs of sentences:

You can go by plane. ...., if that scares you, you can take the train.
Don't forget to take your passport. .... you won't be allowed to cross the frontier.
English people are said to be reserved. .... that applies only to people in the South.
I knew it was probably going to rain. .... I decided to go out for a walk.
If you wait for me I'll give you a lift – .... you'll have to walk all the way.
I knew the plane would be delayed. .... I brought a book to read.
I don't normally like thrillers. .... the one I'm reading now is really good.
We can have French or Spanish food. .... we could go to the Italian restaurant.
I know television is a waste of time. .... I often enjoy watching it.
It's a good idea to write down new words. .... you're likely to forget them.

Unfortunately...

Unfortunately
Fortunately   *Luckily*
Funnily enough   *Strangely enough*   *Believe it or not*
Actually   *In fact*   *In actual fact*
In other words   *That is to say*

Use the adverbs above to connect these sentences:

They fell into the sea. .... neither of them could swim.
I discovered that I'd got no cash with me. .... I had my credit card.
It was nice to see her again. .... we last met when I was still at school.
The party didn't go all that well. .... it was a complete disaster.
I was looking forward to the show. .... I wasn't able to go.
There wasn't much to eat or drink. .... there were only sandwiches and beer.
He can't speak a word of English. .... he speaks fluent Japanese.
The murderer was sent to prison. .... he escaped and hasn't been recaptured.
He spoke too fast and in a strange accent. .... we couldn't understand him at all.
The robbers tied her up and locked her in the cellar. .... she managed to escape.

The reasons why...

1   *In the first place*   2   *In the second place*   *Lastly*
    To begin with   *Secondly*   *Finally*
    First of all   *What's more*
    One reason   *Another reason*
                                Moreover   e.g.   *For example*
                                                          For instance

Look carefully at this example before you start working in pairs:

Importance of accuracy in English: 1 exams (e.g. FCE), 2 writing (e.g. letters)

One reason why accuracy is important is that in many exams, for example in
the First Certificate, inaccuracy can lose marks. Another reason is that if
you're writing, for example a letter, mistakes can give a very bad impression.

Now one of you should look at activity 25 while the other looks at 50.

Write two paragraphs

Write a paragraph or short
story beginning with the scene
on the left and ending with
the scene on the right;
and a paragraph or short
composition on the advantages
and disadvantages of being a
student.

38 PHRASAL AND PREPOSITIONAL VERBS I

Some easy phrasal verbs

These verbs: can be used with   any of these adverbial particles:

come go get climb   *away back*
bring take carry   *past by over round*
pull push   *out off on*
run walk drive ride   *up down in out*
jump fall

Add an appropriate phrasal verb at the end of each of these sentences:

They climbed onto the wall and then they couldn't ...... **get** .. **down**. ....
If you don't want me to stay here, I'll ....
You're standing in my way and I can't ....
The fence was much too high for them to ....
When you've finished with my books, please .... them ....
I felt so dizzy that the whole room seemed to be ....
His finger was stuck in the bottle and he couldn't .... it ....
It's a very annoying dog because it keeps ....
Please .... your muddy boots .... before you come inside.

Some idiomatic prepositional verbs

Fill the gap in each of these sentences with a suitable preposition:

It was easy to see .. **through**. his disguise!
I don't feel .... going out for lunch today.
He's working .... a new book about the supernatural.
She's looking .... someone to look .... her children.
If you ever need a babysitter, just send .... me.
They spent a week in the capital and then made .... the country.
Driving when you're drunk is asking .... trouble.
Young Billy takes .... old Bill, his father.
Those yellow shoes don't go .... your green trousers.
Little Sally looks .... her mother, doesn't she?
The letters FCE stand .... First Certificate in English.
Please get out of the way, I can't see .... you!
Can you call .... me at 8 – I'll be ready.
I find it quite difficult to get used .... foreign food.

Prepositions and particles

*She's going **out**.*
*She's putting **on** her hat.*
*She's putting it **on**.*
*She's putting her hat **on**.* — adverbial particles

*She's looking **in** the mirror.*
*She's looking **in** it.* — prepositions

He wrote down the address. ✓   *She ran down the hill.* ✓
He wrote the address down. ✓   ~~She ran the hill down.~~
He wrote it down. ✓   ~~She ran it down.~~
~~He wrote down it.~~   *She ran down it.* ✓

In each of the following pairs of sentences one is correct and the other is incorrect. Cross out the incorrect sentences.

I can't do without a cigarette.   ~~I can't do a cigarette without.~~
He jumped off the cliff.   He jumped the cliff off.
They opened up them.   They opened up their presents.
He looked the children after.   He looked after them.
I'll play the recording back.   I'll play back it.
It's hard work bringing up children.   It's hard work bringing up them.
The car drove over the bridge.   The car drove the bridge over.
He walked past it.   He walked the shop past.

Rewrite the sentences

Rewrite each sentence so that it means the same, using the phrasal verbs and prepositional verbs on the right.

I asked if he wanted to remove his coat.   take off
Let's raise our glasses and drink to the happy couple.   lift up
I spent a happy hour watching them working.   look at
I'll always regard you as one of my best friends.   look on
Someone has removed my coat from the hall.   take away
Press this button and these little wheels will revolve.   spin round
If necessary you should request further information.   ask for
The firemen managed to extinguish the fire.   put out
Do please visit me if you're in the area.   call on
I found these old school photos in the attic.   come across
I don't like the way he continually stares at me.   keep on
If you know her number you can telephone her.   ring up
If you could wait a moment I'll see if she's available.   hold on
A good friend will always support you.   stand by
Now you've finished you can relax.   sit back

39 PHRASAL AND PREPOSITIONAL VERBS II

Some idiomatic phrasal verbs

The verbs in this exercise are all intransitive (they don't take an object). They are used like this:

Flowers usually come out in the spring.
(**NOT** like this: ~~Flowers usually come in the spring out.~~)

Use the phrasal verbs listed beside each group of sentences to replace the verb in each sentence. You will need to rearrange the phrasal verbs because they are not in the right order. Look at the example first.

The plane left on time. **The plane took off on time.**	stop off/over
We started our journey early in the morning.	take off
We intended to break our journey in Paris.	turn back
There was a thunderstorm but the plane continued flying.	set off/out
But soon the pilot decided to return to London.	fly on

break down	As soon as I arrived at the hotel I registered.
check in	The lift was old and unreliable.
check out	Most days it stopped working after breakfast.
get on	I met some nice people and we were friendly.
get together	We arranged to meet again after our holiday.
wear out	At the end of my stay I left the hotel and paid my bill.

Whenever there are party games I like to participate.	go off
During the party all the lights stopped working.	join in
We continued playing games in the dark.	go off
Suddenly there was a bang like a bomb exploding.	go on
Then the lights all started working again.	carry on/keep on

More idiomatic phrasal verbs

The verbs in this exercise are transitive (they take an object) and are used like this:

Someone has taken my glass away.
Someone has taken away my glass.
Someone has taken it away.
~~Someone has taken away it.~~
My glass has been taken away.

leave on	Let's hear some music on the radio. Can you	
turn up	That's much too loud. Please	
turn down	Oh, the news is on, could you .... now please?	
turn on	Oh dear, the news is so depressing, I'd like you to	
turn off	But if you want to hear it, please do	

	I've got this very complicated form and I've got to	take away
	I've put the wrong date so I'd better	make up
	I can't .... why they want to know all this.	fill in
	I don't know my grandmother's maiden name so I'll just	cross out
	I've had enough of this: could you please	work out

call back	I wanted to .... my meeting with Mr Brown.	
ring back	So I .... first thing in the morning.	
call off	I had to wait while the operator tried to	
ring up	His secretary said he was busy and asked me to	
put off	I told her that I wanted him to .... immediately.	
put through	And then I threatened to .... the whole deal.	

	He's had a nervous breakdown and nobody knows what	give away
	.... four children is an awful strain.	bring on
	And last year he had to .... his evening job.	carry out
	Now someone else will have to .... all his duties.	bring up
	He says he's going to .... all his money.	give up

write down	Chess is a great game – why don't you	
look up	When Mr Brown arrives please	
take up	He looked the wrong way before crossing and I nearly	
show in	Take a piece of paper and .... into four equal-size pieces.	
cut up	If you don't understand this word you'd better	
run over	It'll help you remember these words if you	

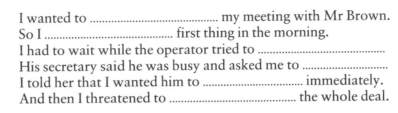
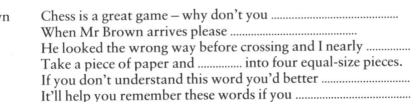

Be + particle

Replace each of the phrases in italics in the sentences with one of the phrases
below, so that the meaning remains the same.

   has finished, has finished, is his responsibility, is out of bed, is cancelled,
   leave, arrive, be published, has gone wrong, take place, be at home, not be at home

Something *is up*, you look worried.
He *is up* all night before an exam.
The lecture *is on* at 7.30.
The party *is over* and it's time to *be off*.
I'll *be out* till 7, then I'll *be in* all evening.

See you later, I'll *be along* about 8.
Your time *is up*, so stop writing now.
It *is up to him* to decide.
The match *is off* because of rain.
His new book *is out* in the spring.

Look at the grammar summary on page 97 for some advice and a warning...

40 WORD ORDER

Modifiers

Look at these examples:

NUMBER	CONDITION, SIZE, etc.	COLOUR	ORIGIN	MATERIAL	PURPOSE	NOUN
One	*brand new*	*pink*	*Swiss*	*woollen*	*ski*	*hat*
Two	*cheap secondhand*	*blue*	*Scottish*	*cotton*	*sun*	*hats*
Three	*large*	*red and yellow*	*American*	*polyester*	*baseball*	*hats*
Four	*ultra-modern*	*orange*	*British-made*	*fibreglass*	*motorcycle*	*helmets*

Now rearrange the words in these phrases:

Five   raincoats   transparent   plastic   large
Six   plants   house   large   bright   green   tropical
Seven   Japanese   white   vases   ceramic   beautiful   flower
Eight   guide   German   old   fascinating   books
Nine   handles   Italian   door   metal   modern
Ten   Swedish   wobbly   bicycles   plastic

Adverbs

Look at the examples, which show where different adverbs can be placed in a sentence. The examples show the 'comfortable' places where they can be placed though other, more emphatic, positions are sometimes possible.

BEFORE	MID	AFTER
Suddenly I had toothache.	*I suddenly had toothache.*	*I had toothache suddenly.*
Yesterday I had toothache.		*I had toothache yesterday.*
Recently I had toothache.	*I recently had toothache.*	*I had toothache recently.*
		I had toothache in bed.
	I certainly had toothache.	
	I never have toothache.	
		I had toothache really badly.

Put the adverbs and adverbial phrases on the right of each sentence into the most 'comfortable' place in the sentence:

I'm going to Italy for my holidays.	probably
She was waiting for me.	indoors
He's leaving the country.	tomorrow
She sings and dances.	beautifully
I stayed in the library and worked.	hard
The door opened and a hand appeared.	slowly
He plays the piano.	very well
You'll have to work to finish on time.	fast
They write to their parents.	weekly
They hid the presents.	behind the sofa

Mid-position adverbs

Adverbs like the ones below often go in mid-position. Look at the examples and notice what is meant by 'mid-position'.

never always often usually once rarely hardly ever frequently ever
obviously clearly surely probably presumably certainly apparently
almost nearly completely just hardly · really

I have never eaten chocolates.
I never eat chocolates.
I can never eat chocolates.
I never have chocolates.
These chocolates will never be eaten.

Put the adverbs on the right into the correct position in each sentence:

I've enjoyed Westerns.	always	He's going to be late.	probably
I've finished my work.	just	I can understand him.	hardly
You'll be met at the airport.	certainly	She loses her temper.	rarely
He shouldn't have done that.	surely	It's very difficult.	obviously
Oops! I fell over.	nearly	Things won't improve.	ever

Rearrange the words

The words in each line below can be rearranged to make a well-known saying. When you have 'solved the puzzles', decide when each saying might be used.

sword the mightier pen than is the
succeed, and if you and don't again at first try try try
world all sorts a takes it to make
well if a thing is it's worth doing doing worth
Rome day built in wasn't a
Rome do when as in do the Romans
milk no use it's spilt over crying
cloud silver has a lining every
end all good must to an things come

Grammar summaries

The language summaries in this section are intended to be used for revision and for quick reference. They offer some useful 'rules of thumb' and examples to help you to remember what you have practised in each unit. They are not supposed to be a substitute for a full-scale grammar reference book and if you need a more detailed explanation of the rules or further examples, you should consult a good grammar book.

---

1 QUESTIONS: *Wh-* and *Yes/No* questions

Question formation:
*What **did** you see yesterday?*
*Who **gave** you this book?*
*Who **did** you **give** that book **to**?*
Did *you see your friends last night?*

Are *you **feeling** all right?*
Is *this correct?*
*How many cakes **have** you **eaten**?*

Different *Wh-* question words:
what, who, where, when, why, what...for, how, how many, how much, which, what else
e.g. **What** *did you do last night?*
What *did you do that **for**?*

Indirect question forms in polite questions:
*Could you tell me **where** the museum **is**?*
*I'd like to know **if** you've **ever been** to London.*
*Would you mind telling me **what** you saw **there**?*

---

2 QUESTIONS: *Isn't it* questions

Negative questions (**making sure** that you are right):
Isn't *that your brother?* ↑ (rising intonation)
Didn't *he once **live** in Spain?* ↑

Question-tags with rising intonation (**finding out** if you are right):
*He used to live in Portugal, **didn't he?** ↑*
*He's older than you, **isn't he?** ↑*
*You haven't got a sister, **have you?** ↑*

Question-tags with falling intonation (**getting agreement** *from your listener*):
*The capital of Portugal is Lisbon, **isn't it?** ↓*
*The weather's improved today, **hasn't it?** ↓*
*It won't rain today, **will it?** ↓*

3 THE PAST: What happened?

Simple past:
   I went to Brazil in 1983.
   I enjoyed my visit to Rio in June.
   I didn't get up till 9 o'clock yesterday morning.

Present perfect:
   Have *you* **ever been** *to Brazil?*
   I've **never been** *to Peru.*
   Have *you* **written** *those letters* yet?

Irregular verbs (see page 6):
   I'd like to **see** *the Amazon.*   *I* **saw** *the Amazon last year.*
   I've never **seen** *the Amazon.*

---

4 THE PAST: What was happening?

The past progressive describes simultaneous activities:
   He **was watching** *TV while you* **were reading.**
   What **were** *you* **doing** *while I* **was waiting** *for you?*

The past progressive also describes actions that began before a point in time and continued after:
   What **were** *you* **doing** *at 9 o'clock this morning?*
   I **was sitting** *in the bath at 8.45.*

The past progressive also describes interrupted actions:
   I **was having** *a bath when the telephone rang.*

Different meanings of the simple past, past progressive and past perfect:
   I **got** *out of bed when the alarm clock went off.*   (after it went off)
   I **was getting** *out of bed when the alarm went off.*   (nearly out of bed)
   I **had got** *out of bed when the alarm went off.*   (no longer in bed)

---

5 PAST, PRESENT AND FUTURE

Talking about recent, current and future events:
   She **has had** *lunch.*   (recently)
   She **is having** *lunch.*   (now)
   She **is going to have** *lunch.*   (soon)

Talking about past activities and habits:
   I once **smoked** *50 cigarettes a week.*   (a long time ago)
   I **used to be** *a heavy smoker.*   (but not any more)
   Did *you* **use to play** *volleyball?*   (when you were younger)

Talking about current habits:
>I **don't smoke** *any more.*
>I *only* **play** *chess now.*

for and *since* + present perfect:
>I *haven't seen him* **since 1980.**   (point in time)
>I *have been feeling unwell* **for several days.**   (period of time)

---

6   SPELLING AND PRONUNCIATION

Vowel sounds (/iː/, /ɪ/, /æ/, /e/, /aː/, /ɒ/, /ʌ/, /ɔː/, /uː/, /ɜː/, /ʊ/)
can be spelt in different ways:
e.g /iː/ *sheep, ceiling, easy, even,* etc.
>/ɒ/ *collar, cough, wash,* etc.

Diphthong sounds (/eɪ/, /əʊ/, /aʊ/, /eə/, /aɪ/, /ɪə/, /ɔɪ/)
can also be spelt in different ways:
e.g. /eɪ/ *tray, eight, lazy, grey, paint,* etc.
>/aɪ/ *buy, high, eye,* **I,** *die, fry,* etc.

Doubling or not doubling consonants:
>*hopping, shopping, travelling, running, quarrelling, letting,* etc.
>*hoping, visiting, offering, benefiting,* etc.

Words written with *ie* and *ei*:
>*believe, field, grief, friend, die, thief, relief,* etc.
>*receive, beige, either, foreign, their, height, leisure, weight,* etc.

---

7   PUNCTUATION

An **apostrophe** (') is used to write contractions (*it's; it isn't; I haven't; he's arrived*) and to make the possessive form of nouns (*the cat's whiskers; John's book; his two sisters' rooms*).

A **comma** (,) is used to separate parts of a sentence that don't identify the subject (*My mother, who is 82, doesn't eat sweets*) but not when one part does identify the other (*The lady who owns the shop is 82*).
It is also used to separate items in a list (*a tall, dark, handsome man; we need eggs, fish, beer and butter*) and before question-tags and forms of address (*It's nice, isn't it? Thanks, John. Please, sir*).
It is also often used to separate an adverbial clause from a main clause (*If it's fine tomorrow, we can go out*) but not when the main clause comes first (*We can go out if it's fine tomorrow*).

Inverted commas (' ' or " ") are used to quote speech (*'That's right,' he said. He said, "That's right."*).

CAPITAL LETTERS are used at the beginning of sentences, and at the beginning of days of the week (*Monday*), months (*July*), public festivals (*Christmas*), nationalities (*British*), languages (*English*), names of people (*Leo Jones*) and their titles (*Uncle John*).
They are also used in some abbreviations (*BBC; HQ; UK; CUP*) but not in others (*e.g.; etc.; i.e.; approx.; max.; min.*).

---

8   POSITION: Place

Prepositions of place:
 in, on, at, behind, in front of, beside, between, among, under,
 underneath, on top of, inside, outside, near to, a long way from
e.g. *The missing wallet was **underneath** a pile of books **behind** my desk.*

Prepositional phrases that describe exact positions:
 on the left of, on the right of, on the left-hand side of, on the side of, on the
 edge of, on the other side of, in the corner of, at the top of, at the bottom of,
 in the middle of, at the back of, at the front of
e.g. *It's **in the corner of** the room, **on the left of** the windowsill.*

---

9   POSITION: Direction and motion

Prepositions of motion and direction:

e.g. *They ran **through** the field and jumped **over** the fence.*
 *Are you going **past** the post office when you come **back from** the bank?*

Describing routes:
 Turn left at...   Turn right at...   Go straight on.
 When you get to the...   When you've passed the...

Verbs of motion used with adverbial particles of direction:
 walk, run, fly, fall, cycle, jump, march, drive, etc.
 across, away, (a)round, past, over, along, in, out, up and down
e.g. *The soldiers **marched past** as the general saluted.*
 *He **walked up and down** outside the examination centre, feeling nervous.*

10   DOING THINGS: Requests and obligation

Making requests:

Would you mind *opening the door?*   **I'd like you to** *open the door.*
Could you *open the door, please?*   *Please* **will you** *open the door?*

Asking for permission:

Would you mind if I *opened the door?*   **May I** *open the door, please?*
Do you mind if I *open the door?*   **Could I** *open the door, please?*

Talking about what is permitted and not permitted (forbidden):

You **can't** *smoke in here.*   *You* **can** *smoke outside.*
You **aren't allowed to** *smoke in here.* *You* **are allowed to** *smoke outside.*

Talking about obligation and lack of obligation:

You **have to** *fill in this form.*   *You* **don't have to** *write in capitals.*
You've **got to** *fill in this form.*   *You* **needn't** *write in capitals.*
You **ought to** *fill in this form.*   **There's no need to** *write in capitals.*

---

11   DOING THINGS: Ability

Ability and inability:

You **can** *swim but I* **can't** *swim.*   **I'm unable to** *swim.*
I'll be able to *swim at the end of the summer.*
I wish I could *swim as well as you can.*
It'd be nice to be able to *swim.*

I **was able to** *jump across the stream.*   *I* **wasn't able to** *step over it.*
I **managed to** *jump across.*   *I* **didn't manage to** *step over.*
I **succeeded in** *jumping across.*   *I* **didn't succeed in** *stepping over.*
(BUT NOT: *I could jump across.*)   *I* **couldn't** *step over.*

Getting help to do things:

I'd need someone to help me *prepare a four-course meal for 12 guests.*
I'd get someone to *do the washing-up afterwards.*
I'd have *the menus printed for me.*

---

12   DOING THINGS: Advice and suggestions

Asking for advice:

Should I **invite** *him to the party?*   *Do you think I should* **invite** *him?*
Is it worth **inviting** *him?*   *Do you think it's worth* **inviting** *him?*
Would it be a good idea **to invite** *him?*   *Do you think it would be a good idea* **to invite** *him?*
Is there any point **in inviting** *him?*   *Do you think there's any point* **in inviting** *him?*
I can't decide whether **to invite** *him.*   *I'm wondering whether* **to invite** *him.*
I can't make up my mind whether **to invite** *him.*

Giving advice and making suggestions:
> *If I were you* **I'd see** *the doctor.*   *You'd better* **see** *him.*
> *I think you* **ought to see** *him.*   *My advice would be* **to see** *him.*
> *Why don't you* **see** *him?*   *It's time you* **saw** *him.*
> *I'd advise you* **to see** *him.*   *It's time you* **decided** *what to do.*
> *It'd be best* **to see** *him.*

Advising against a possible course of action:
> *If I were you I* **wouldn't invite** *her.*   *It'd be better not* **to invite** *her.*
> *I don't think you* **ought to invite** *her.*   *There's no point* **in inviting** *her.*
> *I wouldn't advise you* **to invite** *her.*   *It isn't a good idea* **to invite** *her.*

---

13   VERB + VERB: *-ing* and *to ...*

The *-ing* form is often used as the subject of a sentence:
> **Going** *abroad is pleasant.*   **Being** *criticised is unpleasant.*

to... (the infinitive) is often used after adjectives:
> *It's pleasant* **to go** *abroad.*   *It's unpleasant* **to be** *criticised.*

After a preposition the *-ing* form is always used:
> *He climbed up* **without** *hold**ing** on.*   *He opened it* **by** *hold**ing** it firmly.*

Some verbs are normally followed by the *-ing* form:
> *avoid, enjoy, detest, finish, carry on, etc.*
> e.g. *I* **enjoy** *listen**ing** to music and read**ing** books.*

Some verbs are normally followed by *to...*:
> *choose, learn, manage, mean, need, etc.*
> e.g. *I've* **learnt to** *type and* **to** *do shorthand.*

Some verbs can be followed either by the *-ing* form or by *to...* with no difference in meaning:
> *begin, start, intend, continue, etc.*
> e.g.   *It* **began to** *rain. It* **began** *rain**ing**.*

---

14   VERB +VERB: *-ing, to...* and *that...*

It seems, it appears, it is thought, it is believed can be followed by *to...* or by *that...*:
> *It seems* **to be** *raining.*   *It seems* **that it's** *raining.*
> *It appears* **to have been** *stolen.*   *It appears* **that it has been** *stolen.*

Some verbs are normally only followed by an object + *to...*:
> *He* **encouraged me to** *do it.*   *They* **forced him to** *answer the question.*

Some verbs are normally only followed by *that...*:
> *I* **heard that** *he was in trouble.*   *I* **assume that** *he has been delayed.*

Some verbs can be followed by either *to...* **or** *that...*:
  He's **pretending to** *be stupid.*   *He's* **pretending that** *he's stupid.*

Some verbs can be followed by either an object + the *-ing* form or by *that...*:
  I **noticed them** *watch**ing** me.*   *I* **noticed that** *they were watching me.*

---

15 VERB + VERB: *-ing* or *to ...* ?

Stop + the *-ing* form and *stop* + *to...* have different meanings:
  *He's stopped cough**ing** and sneez**ing**.*   (his cold is better now)
  He stopped **to** *look at the map.*   (he stopped in order to look at the map)

Remember and *forget* can be followed by the *-ing* form or by *to ...* with different meanings:
  *I remember see**ing** her at the party.*   (it is still in my memory)
  I remembered **to** *lock the door.*   (I didn't forget to do that)

Some verbs are followed by the preposition *to* + the *-ing* form:
  I'm **looking forward to** *see**ing** you.*   *I've* **got used to** *be**ing** alone.*

Sorry can be followed by *that...* or by *about* + the *-ing* form:
  I'm sorry **that** *I was rude.*   *I'm sorry* **about** *be**ing** rude.*

Let and *make* are followed by an object + the infinitive (without *to*), while *allow* and *force* are followed by an object + *to...* :
  Please **let me see** *the photos.*   *Please* **allow me to see** *the photos.*
  They **made him confess.**   *They* **forced him to confess.**

---

16 THE FUTURE: Plans and intentions

Different forms are used to talk about future events and activities:
  I'll see you tomorrow.   (promise)
  I'll open the door for you.   (offer)
  I'm **going to** *open this door.*   (intention)
  She's **going to** *have a baby.*   (certainty)
  I'm seeing the dentist tomorrow.   (arrangement)
  Their train **arrives** *at 17.13.*   (timetable)

In a time clause *will* and *going to* are not used:
  I'll have tea when they **arrive.**   *We'll go out if it* **doesn't rain.**

Different verbs can be used to report future plans and intentions:
  He **promised** *to help me.*   *He* **intends** *to go to London next week.*

17 PROBABILITY

Talking about probability and improbability:
    It'll probably *rain.*   **It probably won't** *rain.*
    It looks as if it'll *rain.*   **It doesn't look as if it'll** *rain.*
    It's likely to *rain.*   **It's unlikely to** *rain.*

Talking about certainty and impossibility:
    I'm *absolutely* **sure it'll** *rain.*   **I'm** *absolutely* **sure it won't** *rain.*
    It must be going to *rain.*   **It can't be going to** *rain.*

Talking about possibility or uncertainty:
    It may *rain.*
    There's a chance it'll *rain.*

Judging the truth of statements:
    It's probably *true.*   **It can't be** *true.*   **It sounds as if it's** *true.*

Judging the likelihood of events having happened in the past:
    It probably *happened.*   **It can't have** *happened.*   **It's unlikely to have** *happened.*

---

18 COMPARISON

The use of the comparative (*better, more interesting*, etc.):
    Brazil is **much larg**e**r than** *Greece.*   *Greece isn't* **as** *cold* **as** *Canada.*
    Canada is **less** *humid* **than** *Japan.*   *Japan is* **more** *mountainous* **than** *Ireland.*

The use of the superlative (*best, most interesting*, etc.):
    Jim is **the** *fattest boy in the class.*   *He's also* **the least** *intelligent.*

so, such a, too and *enough* are used in 'result-clauses':
    The box is **so** *heavy* **that** *I can't lift it.*   *It's* **too** *heavy for me* **to** *lift.*
    It's **such a** *heavy box* **that** *I can't lift it.*   *It's* **not** *light* **enough** *for me* **to** *lift.*

---

19 REPORTED SPEECH: Statements

Statements made recently are normally reported with present tense verbs:
    'I'm feeling sick. → *He* **says** **that** *he's feeling sick.*
    'It's too difficult. → *He* **think**s **that** *it's too difficult.*

Statements made some time ago are reported with past tense verbs:
    'It'll be difficult.' →*He* **said that** *it* **would** *be difficult.*
    'It's a long way.' → *He* **told me that** *it* **was** *a long way.*

20 REPORTED SPEECH: Questions and requests

Questions are reported with a change in word-order from direct speech:
'Is this true?' → *He asked me* **if it was** *true.*
'When is it going to happen?' → *He wanted to know* **when it was** *going to happen.*

Requests, orders, advice and invitations are reported using *to...* :
'Please open the door.' → *She asked me* **to** *open the door.*
'You should stop smoking.' → *She advised me* **to** *stop smoking.*
'Would you like to come?' → *She invited me* **to** *come.*

---

21 PREPOSITIONAL PHRASES I

Preposition + noun expressions (see pages 42– 43):
in bed, in pencil   *by heart, by accident*
on holiday, on purpose   *at home, at school*
out of date, out of sight etc.
e.g *I lay* **in** *bed* **at** *home trying to learn the words* **by** *heart.*

Prepositional phrases are used to describe different ways of travelling:
for a drive, for a walk   *on a journey, on a trip*
by car, by train   *on a train, on a bus*
on the train, on the bus   *in a train, in a bus*
in the train, in the bus   etc.
e.g. *Normally I come* **by** *bus/***in the** *bus/***on the** *bus, but today I came* **on** *foot.*

---

22 PREPOSITIONAL PHRASES II

Prepositional phrases with *time* (see page 44):
on time, in time, before my time, behind the times, etc.
e.g. *He never arrives* **on** *time.*   *He arrived* **in** *time for the meal.*

Preposition + noun + preposition expressions (see page 44):
in addition to, in time for, in charge of, etc.
e.g. *Bill's* **in** *charge* **of** *the office while the boss is away.*

Some prepositional phrases can be used to connect sentences:
on the one hand ... on the other hand, for example, in theory, etc.
e.g. *What you said was interesting.* **In theory** *you're right, but* **on the other hand** *you should realise that...*

23 ARTICLES: *a, the* or *Ø*?

The use of articles to refer to things in general or in particular:

I wish I had **a** *banana or* **an** *orange.*	(any one)
I love bananas and oranges.	(in general)
The *banana I had was nasty but* **the** *orange was nice.*	(in particular)
Would you like **some** *bananas or* **some** *other fruit?*	(any ones)
Fruit is good for you and bananas are best of all.	(in general)
I enjoy music and writing letters.	(in general)

a(n) is used before names of professions but not before subjects studied:
   I want to be **a** *doctor. That's why I'm studying medicine.*

the or *a* are left out in some prepositional phrases:
   You should go **to bed.**   *He's* **at work.**
but not in other prepositional phrases:
   Stop looking out of **the** *window.*   *I got this at* **a** *shop near me.*

Most place names do not have *the* at the beginning:
   Britain, Cambridge, Oxford Street, etc.
   BUT: **the** *USA,* **the** *Soviet Union,* **the** *UK,* **the** *Atlantic,* **the** *Alps,* etc.

---

24 *If* SENTENCES: Types 1 and 2

If can be used in three different types of conditional sentences:
1 *If I* **see** *him, I'll* **tell** *him.*   (I may see him)
   If I **don't see** *him, I* **won't tell** *him.*   (I may not see him)
2 *If he* **was/were** *clever, he'd/he* **would** *pass the exam.*   (he isn't clever)
   If she **wasn't** *stupid, she* **wouldn't** *fail.*   (she is stupid)
3 *If I* **had** *known, I'd/I* **would have** *told him.*   (I didn't know)
   If we **hadn't** *been silly, we* **wouldn't have** *done that.*   (we were silly)

If, unless, when and *till/until* have different meanings:
   I'll make tea **when** *they arrive.*   (they will arrive sooner or later)
   I'll make tea **if** *they arrive.*   (but they may not come)
   I won't make tea **until** *they arrive.*   (not before they come)
   I won't make tea **unless** *they arrive.*   (but they may not come at all)

---

25 *If* SENTENCES: Type 3

In Type 3 conditionals *had* and *would* can both be contracted to *'d*:
   If I'd known (**had** *known), I'd have* (I **would have**) *told you about it.*

Sometimes 'mixed' conditionals can be formed from Types 2 and 3:
   If I **had been** *born 100 years ago, I* **wouldn't be** *here today.*
   If they **weren't** *so stupid, they* **wouldn't have** *made those mistakes.*

26 RELATIVE CLAUSES

'Identifying' relative clauses are formed using *who, that, which, where* or *whose*:

    He is the man **who** *I told you about.*   *He is the man* **that** *I told you about.*
    This is the thing **which** *you need.*   *This is the thing* **that** *you need.*
    She's the girl **whose** *father won the prize.*
    He has two sons: the son **who** *is a*
      doctor lives in London.

who, that and *which* can be left out if they are the object of an 'identifying' relative clause:

    He is the man I told you about.   *This is the thing you need.*

'Non-identifying' relative clauses are formed using *who, which, where, when* or *whose:*

    My mother, **who** *is 67, likes sweets.*   *My house,* **which** *is old, is falling to pieces.*
    1812, **when** *Napoleon went to Russia, was a very significant year.*

who and *which* can be used to connect sentences:

    She is very shy, **which** *I find surprising.*
    I'm in love with Chris, **who** *is a wonderful person.*

('Identifying' relative clauses contain essential information. 'Non-identifying' relative clauses contain extra non-essential information, sometimes added as an afterthought. Notice the use of **commas** in writing such sentences.)

---

27 ADJECTIVES AND VERBS + PREPOSITION I

Some adjectives are normally followed by *at*:

    Good at, brilliant at, terrible at, hopeless at, etc.
e.g *She's good* **at** *tennis but hopeless* **at** *other sports.*

Some adjectives are normally followed by *about* or by *of*:

    angry about, happy about, nervous about, etc.
    afraid of, terrified of, scared of, etc.
e.g. *I'm worried* **about** *the future.*   *I'm scared* **of** *flying.*

Some adjectives are followed by particular prepositions:

    unkind to, responsible for, proud of, impressed by/with, sorry for/about, etc.
e.g. *She is very unkind* **to** *her son.*   *I feel sorry* **for** *people with no homes.*

Some verbs are followed by particular prepositions:

    succeed in, consist of, depend on, belong to, etc.
e.g. *Her future depends* **on** *her exam results.*   *She succeeded* **in** *passing.*

28 ADJECTIVES AND VERBS + PREPOSITION II

Some verbs are followed by a preposition + object or by an indirect object:
> *give, sell, lend, bring, return, offer, deliver, give back, take,* etc.

e.g. *He gave the books* **to me.**   *He gave* **me** *the books.*
> *He took the money* **from** *the bank.*

Some verbs are followed by particular prepositions:
> *look for, stare at, dream of/about, look after, look at,* etc.

e.g. *I'm looking* **for** *my lost cat.*   *I'll look* **after** *her while you're away.*

---

29 THE PASSIVE

Different forms of the passive:
> *'Hamlet'* **was written** *by Shakespeare.*   (Shakespeare wrote 'Hamlet'.)
> *I think I'm* **being followed.**   (I think someone is following me.)
> **Being laughed at** *is unpleasant.*   (It's unpleasant if someone laughs at you.)
> *He* **has been arrested.**   (The police have arrested him.)

The passive is sometimes used to describe actions where the person responsible is unknown or unimportant:
> *He* **has been** *murdered.*   (but I don't know who by)
> *He* **was jailed** *for three months.*   (by the judge, obviously)

It is also used to place important new information at the end of a sentence:
> *Today's sunny, warm weather will be followed tomorrow* **by rain.**
> *Did you know that I was met at the airport* **by a dozen people?**

---

30 WORD FORMATION: Adjectives and adverbs

Adjectives can be formed from nouns or verbs by adding one of the following endings *-y, -able, -al, -ive, -ful* and *-ish*:
> *cloud – cloudy, wool – woolly*   *read – readable, advise – advisable*
> *logic – logical, habit – habitual*   *attract – attractive, explode – explosive*
> *care – careful, pain – painful*   *young – youngish, red – reddish,* etc.

Opposites of adjectives ending in *-y* can be formed with *-less* or with *un-*:
> *painful – painless, careful – careless, harmful – harmless,* etc.
> *helpful –* **un**helpful, *successful –* **un**successful, *truthful –* **un**truthful, etc.

Adverbs are formed from adjectives by adding *-ly*:
> *happy – happily, slow – slowly, careful – carefully,* etc.

(BUT notice these exceptions:
> *hard, fast, well, late, early*
> *in a lovely way, in a silly way, in a friendly way, in a lonely way*)

31   WORD FORMATION: Verbs

Verbs can be formed from some adjectives by adding *-en*:
   tight – to *tighten*, flat – to *flatten*, loose – to *loosen*, etc.
but other similar verbs are formed in different ways:
   pure – to **puri**fy, *cool* – to **cool**, *hot* – to **heat**, *large* – to **en**large, etc.

Verbs with **un-** are sometimes the opposite of phrasal verbs with *up*:
   unscrew – screw **up**, **un**button – button **up**, *unzip* – zip **up**, etc.

Some verbs can be formed from other verbs with *over-* and *mis-*:
   eat – **over**eat, *sleep* – **over**sleep, *work* – **over**work, etc.
   understand – **mis**understand, *behave* – **mis**behave, etc.

---

32   WORD FORMATION: Abstract nouns

Nouns can be formed from adjectives by adding *-ness, -ity, -ence* and *-y*:
   polite – polite**ness**, *happy* – happi**ness**, *tidy* – tidi**ness**, etc.
   stupid – stupid**ity**, *certain* – certain**ty**, *popular* – popular**ity**, etc.
   violent – viol**ence**, *patient* – pati**ence**, *intelligent* – intellig**ence**, etc.
   honest – hones**ty**, *accurate* – accura**cy**, *anxious* – anxi**ety**, etc.
but other similar nouns are formed in different ways:
   strong – **strength**, *bored* – bore**dom**, *brave* – brave**ry**, etc.

Nouns can be formed from verbs by adding *-ment, -ion, -ation, -ance, -ence* and
-al:

   announce – announce**ment**, etc.   *discuss* – discuss**ion**, etc.
   admire – admir**ation**, etc.   *perform* – perform**ance**, etc.
   insist – insist**ence**, etc.   *refuse* – refus**al**, etc.

(See communication activities 30, 40, 52 and 55 for more examples.)

---

33   WORD FORMATION: Opposites

Negative forms of adjectives, nouns and verbs can be formed with *un-, in-, im-,*
in-, ir-, dis- and *non-:*
   unlikely, **un**comfortable   **in**accurate, **in**tolerant
   impossible, **im**moral (+ p or m)   **il**legal, **il**logical (+ l)
   irregular, **ir**relevant (+ r)   **dis**obedient, **dis**agree
   non-smoker, **non**-stick   etc.

But many common nouns have opposites that are not formed with prefixes:
   happy – sad, *warm* – cool, *gentle* – rough, *brave* – cowardly, etc.

(See communication activity 42 for more examples.)

34   QUANTITY AND NUMBERS

Some nouns are 'countable':
   car(s), fact(s), person/people, hour(s), bottle(s), slice(s), etc.
e.g.   *How **many** cars can you see?*
   *That **is an** interesting fact.*

Other nouns are 'uncountable':
   traffic, information, work, time, beer, bread, etc.
e.g.   *How **much** traffic **is** there on the road?*
   *This **is** interesting information.*   (**but:** *This is **an** interesting **piece of**
   information.*)
   *There was **so much** work to do.*   (**but:** *I'd like **a bottle of** beer.*)

Numbers spoken aloud and written out in full:
   14 fourteen;
   44 forty-four;
   440 four hundred and forty;
   4,400 four thousand four hundred;
   4,400,000 four million, four hundred thousand, etc.

Arithmetical symbols:
   + plus;
   − minus;
   × times/multiplied by;
   ÷ divided by;
   = equals;
   3^2 *three squared,* etc.

---

35   JOINING SENTENCES I

Different verb forms used with *when* in time clauses:
   *I **spoke** to him when he **arrived**.*
   *I'**ll speak** to him when he **arrives**.*
   *I **started** my dinner when he **left/had left**.*   (He left, then I started)
   *I **had started** dinner when he **left**.*   (I started, then he left)

Different time-conjunctions can be used in time clauses:
   as, until/till, by the time, whenever, while, as soon as, since, etc.
e.g.   *He rang me up **as** I was having breakfast.*
   *I feel sick **whenever** I have to do an exam.*

Time-prepositions can also be used in a similar way:
   during, before, since, after, till/until
e.g.   *He rang me up **during** breakfast.*
   *I always feel sick **before** an exam.*

36   JOINING SENTENCES II

Conjunctions can be used to join sentences in different ways:
I've brought my umbrella **in case** *it rains.*   (precaution)
I've got my umbrella **because/as** *it's raining.*   (reason)
You don't need an umbrella **unless** *it's raining.*   (condition)
I've got an umbrella **so that** *I don't get wet.*   (purpose)
I've brought an umbrella **although** *it's not raining.*   (contrast)

Related nouns or pronouns can be connected with co-ordinating structures:
Both *Bill* **and** *his sister came.*   *Bring* **either** *wine* **or** *beer.*
Neither *John* **nor** *Mary came.*   **None of** *the family came* **except** *Ivy.*

---

37   JOINING SENTENCES III: Links between sentences

Time adverbs can be used to link two separate sentences together:
He left at 6.30. **Before that** *we'd had a long talk.*
She had a lovely time at the party. **Meanwhile** *I was at home studying.*
We had a superb meal. **Afterwards** *we had to do the washing-up.*

Other adverbial phrases can be used to link two separate sentences together in a similar way:
I hate bananas. **That's why** *I never eat fruit salad.*   (reason)
I love oranges. **Nevertheless** *I hate having to peel them.*   (contrast)
You could have ice cream. **On the other hand** *you could have fruit.*   (alternative)

Some adverbial phrases can be used to connect several sentences together in a paragraph:
In the first place *I don't like cooking very much.* **In fact,** *I hate it.*
What's more *I find that spending hours in the kitchen is exhausting.*

(See pages 74–75 for complete lists of adverbial phrases and adverbs.)

38   PHRASAL AND PREPOSITIONAL VERBS I

Phrasal verbs are used differently from prepositional verbs:
> *I put* **on** *my coat. I put my coat* **on**. *I put it* **on**. (BUT NOT: *I put on it*)
> *He jumped* **off** *the cliff. He jumped* **off** *it.* (BUT NOT: *He jumped it off*
> NOR: *He jumped the cliff off*)

put on is a phrasal verb (= verb + adverbial particle);
jump off is a prepositional verb (= verb + preposition) but it can also be used as
a phrasal verb: *He jumped off.*

Phrasal verbs can be formed with verbs of motion + adverbial particles:
> VERBS: *jump, run, come, climb, drive, pull, push, bring* etc.
> ADVERBIAL PARTICLES: *off, out, past, down, up, away, back, in, over,* etc.
> e.g. *The general saluted as the soldiers* **marched past.**
> *Please* **go away** *and don't* **come back.**

Many prepositional verbs are used idiomatically (you can't work out their
meaning from their parts):
> *I* **saw through** *his disguise.*   (I wasn't fooled by it)
> *He* **takes after** *his father.*   (He behaves in the same way as him)
> *I'll* **call for** *you at 7.30.*   (I'll come to your house to fetch you)

Some advice and a warning
The phrasal verbs (and prepositional verbs) in this unit and unit 39 are a small
selection of thousands of similar verbs in English. You need to *understand* many
of these but in many cases you don't need to learn to *use* them. It's tempting to
try to be terribly 'English' and to talk as idiomatically as possible, but foreigners
are *not expected* to use idiomatic English – in fact native speakers sometimes
find that foreigners using idioms sound rather funny!
It's best, therefore, to concentrate on using just a few essential phrasal verbs (the
ones in these units) and to make sure you understand the others when you hear
them being used.

---

39   PHRASAL AND PREPOSITIONAL VERBS II

Many idiomatic phrasal verbs are 'inseparable' and are not followed by an
object:
> *The plane* **took off** *on time.*   *Roses* **come out** *in the summer.*
> *My shoes are* **worn out.**   *Let's* **get together** *next week.*

Other idiomatic phrasal verbs are followed by an object:
> *Please* **take** *this soup* **away.**   *Please* **take away** *this soup.*
> *He* **turned** *the radio* **on.**   *He* **turned on** *the radio.*

Some phrasal verbs are formed from **to be** + particle:
> *It's time for me to* **be off.**   *The war* **was over.**
> *I'll* **be along** *later.*   *Your time* **is up** *now.*

40   WORD ORDER

Adjectives and other words that come before a noun are arranged in this order:
   1 number, 2 size or condition, 3 colour, 4 origin, 5 material,
   6 purpose, 7 the noun itself
e.g. *two beautiful brown Greek woollen fisherman's jerseys.*

Some adverbs are normally placed in 'mid-position' in a sentence:
   I have **never** *eaten oysters.*   *I can* **never** *eat oysters.*
   I **never** *eat oysters.*   *I'll* **never** *eat oysters.*
(similarly used adverbs are: *always, often, almost, hardly, rarely,* etc. – see page 81)

Other adverbs may fit more comfortably at the beginning or end of a sentence:
   Yesterday *I went to the zoo*   *I went to the zoo* **yesterday.**
   Recently *I went to the city.*   *I went to the city* **recently.**
but some of these adverbs may also fit in mid-position:
   I **recently** *went to the city.*

(It is best to rely on your own feelings for what sounds right or comfortable, rather than to try to memorise the complex rules of word order.)

Communication activities

Answer your partner's questions about the photo below. Then get ready to ask your partner questions about his or her photo.

1

Imagine that you have been shopping to get the items on the left-hand list of page 22. Unfortunately, you haven't been able to get exactly what was required. Tell your partner about this and find out what he or she managed to get from the other list.

2

12 eggs (size 3) — only size 4 available, got those
1 kg carrots ✓
3 large tins beans — None in shop, not even small tins
1 jar marmalade — No, got apricot jam instead
2 small wholemeal
  loaves — No, got 1 large one
2 packets chocolate
  biscuits — No
1 jar instant coffee — special offer: got 2 for the price of one!

3 Ask each of your partners for the following information:

favourite film star   favourite food
place of birth   what time they left home today
mother's first name   when they usually have dinner
favourite sport

Don't make any notes, but rely on your memory. It's your turn *second*.
Later you'll have to check with your partners whether you can remember the information correctly, by asking questions like this:
'Your favourite film star is Burt Reynolds, isn't he?'

4 Dictate the words below to your partner. Say each word twice but don't spell them out letter by letter. Check your partner's spelling in each list.

/i:/	/ɪ/	/æ/	/e/	/a:/	/ɒ/	/ʌ/	/ɔ:/
easy	quick	lamp	bread	glass	wrong	trouble	walk
breathe	busy	marriage	cheque	heart	wasp	blood	nought
even	village	canteen	health	disaster	knock	money	daughter

/u:/	/ɜ:/	/ʊ/
loose	shirt	wool
suitable	worm	butcher
screw	firm	pudding

5 Find out if your partner has ever done any of the things shown below. If the answer is *Yes*, then find out *When...?*
and *What was it like?*
and *What happened exactly?*

Ever ridden a racing bike?
been to London?
been caught in a dust storm?
eaten lobster?
drunk sherry?
visited a Latin American country?
been involved in a motor accident?
voted in an election?

Ever driven a delivery van?
been skiing?
tried surfing?
read a book by John le Carré?
been stopped by the police?
been taken to hospital?
won a race or a competition?
baked a cake?

(When answering your partner's questions, it may be more enjoyable to tell lies and pretend that you really did, for example, get bitten by a dog once.)

6

Find out about your partner's photo by asking questions. Then answer his or her questions about the photo below.

7

All the items listed are normally allowed as hand luggage without extra charge except for: animals (any size), briefcase (this would count as a second handbag), skis.

You are allowed to: drink and eat during the flight, undo your seat belt after take-off, go to sleep, walk about during the flight, smoke cigarettes (but only when NO SMOKING sign is off and in a smoking seat).
You're not allowed to: smoke in the toilet, smoke in the aisle, stand up during take-off or landing, open a door or window, smoke a pipe, run up and down the aisle.

8

Give the following instructions to your partner, using the expressions suggested on page 20.

Raise both your hands to shoulder level. Put them both out in front of you. Now put them behind your neck. Stand up. Put your left hand on your right shoulder. Put your right hand on your left hip. Turn round slowly 2½ times until you're facing the other way. Wink with your left eye. Then with your other eye. Whistle or hum the first line of 'Happy Birthday to You'. Sit down again. Let both arms drop to your sides. Relax both arms. Close your eyes. Open them very wide. Look at me without smiling for 30 seconds. Fine, now relax, thank you.

Now follow your partner's instructions.

9

Ask each of your partners for the following information:
favourite singer or musician   favourite city or town
name of street they live in   name of best friend
names of brothers or sisters   lucky number
what time they got up this morning

Don't make any notes, but rely on your memory. It's your turn *last*.
Later you'll have to check with your partners whether you can remember the
information correctly by asking questions like this:
'You got up at 7 this morning, didn't you?'

10

Dictate each short list to your partner, saying each word twice. Don't spell any
words out letter by letter. Check your partner's spelling.

/eɪ/	/əʊ/	/aʊ/	/eə/	/aɪ/	/ɪə/	/ɔɪ/
grey	boast	crowd	scarce	shiny	appear	destroy
lazy	joke	trousers	various	thigh	merely	moisture
favour	though	proud	repair	bike	theory	poison

11

Starting in the top left-hand corner of the cartoon and going clockwise, explain
to your partner the route his or her pen should take (on page 18) to draw the
same figure. Make sure your partner draws the figure in exactly the way shown.
Don't tell your partner what the figure is going to be!

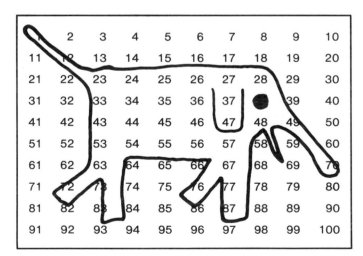

12

Ask each of your partners for the following information:

favourite colour   favourite drink
birthday   how they came to school
father's first name   what their jobs are
hobbies

Don't make any notes, but rely on your memory. It's your turn *first*.
Later you'll have to check with your partners whether you can remember the
information correctly, by asking questions like this:

'Your favourite colour's pink, isn't it?'

13

Imagine that you have been shopping to get the items on the right-hand list on
page 22. Unfortunately, you haven't been able to get exactly what was required.
Tell your partner about this and find out what he or she managed to get from
the left-hand list.

1 large roll sticky tape — had to get 2 small rolls
1 box paper clips ✓
2 cassettes (C90) — got 3 C60s instead
2 red ballpoints — no, but got 1 blue one
4 size AA alkaline batteries — no, but got cheaper ones
1 packet airmail envelopes — no, only ordinary ones, so didn't get any
1 large glue stick ✓ (but have lost it!)

14

Look at the sketch below. Describe it to your partner simply enough for him
or her to draw it, following your instructions. Later you'll have to listen to a
description of your partner's sketch and draw that.

15 Find out if your partner has ever done any of the things shown below. If the answer is *Yes*, then find out *When...?*
and *What was it like?*
and *What happened exactly?*

Ever ridden a motorbike?
been abroad?
been caught in a thunderstorm?
eaten snails?
failed an exam?
tried wind-surfing?
read a book by Hemingway?
been scratched by a cat?

Ever drunk champagne?
cooked a meal for a family?
visited a Mediterranean country?
driven a fast car?
been water-skiing?
been given a marvellous present?
been bitten by a dog?
found some money in the street?

(When answering your partner's questions, it may be more enjoyable to tell lies and pretend that you really did, for example, win a competition once.)

16 Get your partner to do the sums below on a scrap of paper if necessary, or using a calculator perhaps. Explain what he or she has to do step by step.

2×14 $(= 28)$; $+ 12$ $(= 40)$; $\div 5$ $(= 8)$; $\times 10$ $(= 80)$;

$- 13$ $(= 67)$; -1 $(= 66)$; $\div 11$ $(= 6)$; $- 4$ ('And what's the answer?')

17 Dictate or spell aloud each of the names in the first column and ask your partner to write them down. Check his or her spelling.
The names in the second column are the names these people are better known as – see if your partner can guess any of this information.

Issur Danielovitch Demsky (Kirk Douglas)
Marion Michael Morrison (John Wayne)
Raquel Tejada (Raquel Welch)
Bernard Schwarz (Tony Curtis)
Lucius Domitius Ahenobarbus (Nero)
Reginald Dwight (Elton John)
Robert Zimmermann (Bob Dylan)

18

As you can see, there is some information missing from the lists below. Here are some questions you can ask your partner to find out if he or she has the missing information:

Who was born in ...?   When did ... die?
Who died in ...?   When was ... born?

You can also ask questions like these to test your partner's general knowledge:

What did ... do in his life?
What did ... become famous for?
What is ... remembered for still today?

Births		Deaths	
1770	Beethoven		Beethoven
1853		1890	van Gogh
1874	Winston Churchill	1945	
1879	Einstein +		Stalin
1881	Picasso	1955	Einstein
1889	Charlie Chaplin	1963	
	+ Adolf Hitler		Churchill
	John F. Kennedy	1973	Picasso
1935	Elvis Presley	1977	Chaplin +

19

Follow the instructions your partner gives you, first. Then give the following instructions to your partner, using the expressions suggested on page 20.

Raise your right hand. Place it on your left knee. Lift your left leg 10 cm from the floor. Stand up. Remove your right hand from your knee. Place your right hand on your right hip. Now put both feet on the floor. Keep both feet pressed closely together. Let your left hand fall loose. Wave your left hand loosely by your side. Do the same with your other hand. Keep both arms waving loosely and sit down. Now keep completely still for 30 seconds without blinking. Relax, thank you.

20

Dictate the words below to your partner. Say each word twice but don't spell them out letter by letter. Check your partner's spelling in each list.

/iː/	/ɪ/	/æ/	/e/	/aː/	/ɒ/	/ʌ/	/ɔː/
clean	women	lamb	breath	grass	watch	cousin	law
knee	filthy	damage	check	calm	squash	tough	naughty
eager	silly	scandal	guess	bargain	knob	stomach	cautious

/uː/	/ɜː/	/ʊ/
juice	bird	should
truth	search	bull
tool	worth	cushion

21

Dictate or spell aloud each of the names in the first column and ask your partner to write them down. Check his or her spelling.

The names in the second column are the names by which these people are better known — see if your partner can guess any of this information.

Walter Matuschanskavasky	(Walter Matthau)
Maurice Mickelwhite	(Michael Caine)
Eric Arthur Blair	(George Orwell)
Kyriakos Theotokopoulos	(El Greco)
Richard Starkie	(Ringo Starr)
Sophia Scicoloni	(Sophia Loren)
Roy Scherer Fitzgerald	(Rock Hudson)
Archibald Leach	(Cary Grant)

22

Find out from your partner what everyone is doing in the scene he or she is looking at. Ask what has happened, what the people did earlier and what they are going to do next.

Then tell your partner about the scene below and what you think the people did earlier and what they are going to do later.

Describe these three uncles to your partner, using these structures:
Both Uncle Dave and Uncle Frank ...
Neither Uncle Eric nor Uncle Frank ...
Uncle Dave hasn't got either a ... or a ...

23

DAVE   ERIC   FRANK

Dictate each short list to your partner, saying each word twice. Don't spell any words out letter by letter. Check your partner's spelling.

24

/eɪ/	/əʊ/	/aʊ/	/eə/	/aɪ/	/ɪə/	/ɔɪ/
shame	ghost	drown	rarely	bright	serious	choice
ache	folk	mountain	fairy	guide	beard	enjoyable
paint	moan	frown	spare	delighted	sphere	noise

Tell your partner the advantages/disadvantages of the following activities. Where you have advantages to talk about, your partner has disadvantages and vice versa.

25

```
REASONS FOR KEEPING A DOG:  1 faithful
   2 obedient
   3 good companion
REASONS FOR NOT GOING ABROAD ON A COACH TOUR:  1 don't see the real country
   2 stuck with strangers
   3 treated like a sheep
REASONS FOR GOING TO LIVE ABROAD:  1 you can see the real country
   2 independent from family
   3 you can learn the language
REASONS FOR NOT BUYING A TELEVISION:  1 most programmes are terrible (e.g.
   soap operas, quiz shows)
   2 better news coverage in the papers
   3 no time for other pastimes
REASONS FOR OWNING A CAR:  1 independence (e.g. go where and when you like)
   2 enjoyment of driving
   3 friends who need lifts
```

26

As you can see, there is some information missing from the lists below. Here are some questions you can ask your partner to find out if he or she has the missing information:

Who was born in ...? When did ... die?
Who died in ...? When was ... born?

You can also ask questions like these to test your partner's general knowledge:

What did ... do in his life?
What did ... become famous for?
What is ... remembered for still today?

Births		Deaths	
	Beethoven	1827	Beethoven
1853	van Gogh	1890	
1874		1945	Adolf Hitler
1879	Einstein + Stalin	1953	Stalin
	Picasso		Einstein
1889	Charlie Chaplin	1963	Kennedy
	+	1965	Churchill
1917	John F. Kennedy		Picasso
1935			Chaplin + Presley

27

Look at the sketch below. Later you'll have to describe it to your partner. But first listen to your partner's description of another sketch and, following the instructions, draw it yourself.

Imagine that you and your partner have stocked up with provisions for a camping holiday. Find out what your partner still has left and tell him or her what you have left. Follow this pattern:

A: Have you got any ....*rice*........ left?

B: Yes. How much would you like? OR How many ....*packet*....s would you like?

A: .*Four*......., please.

B: I'm sorry, I've only got ..*two*......   OR   Here you are!

28

Things you have run out of	Things you still have left
beer	lemonade (12)
bread	sugar (2)
chocolate	matches (4)
cigarettes	toothpaste (4)
honey	milk (½)
rice	salt (1)

Ask your partner to react to each of the following promises, threats and offers using the expressions shown on page 59.

29

If you like I'll ...
  send you a postcard.
  tell you a story.
  give you a cake.
  drive you to the airport.
  wake you up at 6 am.

If we're not careful someone will ...
  punish us.
  shout at us.
  give us extra work to do.
  tell us off.

30

arrive	arrival		die	death		complain	complaint
survive	survival		be born	birth		obey	obedience
approve	approval		prove	proof		break	breakage
perform	performance		laugh	laughter		sign	signature
disappear	disappearance		lose	loss		succeed	success
assist	assistance		choose	choice			
resist	resistance		behave	behaviour			
insist	insistence		fail	failure			
prefer	preference		please	pleasure			
persist	persistence		believe	belief			

31

Rewrite this reported conversation in dialogue form, showing only the names of the speakers (Dan and Kate) and giving the exact words they are supposed to have said.

> I mentioned to Kate that I was seeing Lucy and she immediately told me to ring her up and break everything off. I was pretty shocked, I can tell you, and I said she had no right to tell me how to organise my private life. She just laughed and told me not to be silly. Well of course, I told her to get out and leave me alone. At first she tried to refuse but in the end I persuaded her to go.

32

Tell your partner what everyone is doing in this scene. Describe what you think has happened, what the people did earlier and what they are going to do later.

Then find out about your partner's scene, asking what happened earlier and what's going to happen next.

33

Part 1

You're going to do several things that may get on your partner's nerves. Continue doing each thing shown here until you're asked to stop:

> whistle   whisper to yourself   sigh   sniff   clear your throat

If your partner's actions get on your nerves, ask him or her to stop by saying:

> 'Please stop whistling,' or 'Please don't go on whistling.'

Part 2

Imagine that you're talking to your partner about a long walk you once went on. You had to make several stops on the way and you may need to explain these:

1st stop: drink	4th stop: meal
2nd stop: looked at map	5th stop: met a friend
3rd stop: made a phone call	6th stop: bought some sweets

Your conversation should go like this:

A: Why did you make your first stop?
B: I stopped to pick a flower.
A: I see, and then what?
B: After picking the flower I went on walking but I soon stopped again.
A: Why did you stop again?

34

Imagine that you ran into an old friend, Mary, the other day, She told you all about her husband, John. This is what she said to you.

'John and I have been together for eight years.
We first got to know each other at a Christmas party.
But we had seen each other a couple of times before that.
He had just arrived when he asked me to dance with him.
We danced all night and left the party at dawn.
I told him that I didn't really like parties or dancing.
We went out together every evening that week.
We got engaged in July or August the same year.
I'll never forget our honeymoon – two weeks of uninterrupted rain!
And we've managed to stay together ever since – in spite of having
    rows and arguments practically every week!'

Report this conversation to your partner, who has been talking to John.

35

Anne wears glasses.	Belinda was in your class at school.
Elizabeth plays tennis.	Hazel used to sing in a rock group.
Carole has long fair hair.	Dawn used to be a fashion model.
Gwen has a young baby.	Fanny was your sister's best friend at school.

36

See if you can guess the causes of each event on the left. Your partner knows the right answers. Then see if your partner can guess the causes of the events on the right.

Alex is wearing someone else's shoes.

Bob is looking very happy.

Chris hasn't shaved this morning.

David was late for work every day last week.

Little Emma is crying because her mummy smacked her for hitting her brother.

Frank is very tired because he stayed up all night reading an exciting book.

George has a broken arm because he fell off his bike.

Hilda was late for work every day last week for these reasons:

Mon. trains on strike
Tue. overslept
Wed. missed train
Thu. got on wrong train
Fri. took morning off as holiday

37

Don Quixote has a dream of being a perfect knight.

In *The Grapes of Wrath* a family leave Oklahoma to find work in California.

In *Babes in the Wood* two children find a house made of gingerbread.

Citizen Kane's dying word is 'Rosebud'.

E.T. is a creature from outer space.

King Kong, an enormous animal, is captured on a remote island.

38

Part 1

These are some things you were supposed to do, which you either remembered to do (✓) or forgot to do (✗).

post letter ✗   buy newspaper ✓   go to bank ✗   get petrol ✓   buy stamps ✗

Find out if your partner did these things that he or she promised to do:

do the shopping   phone hairdresser   prepare lesson   collect dry-cleaning   write composition

Use some of these phrases in your conversation:

Did you remember to...?   I'm afraid I forgot to...   I did remember to...
I expect you forgot to...   I didn't remember to...   I didn't forget to...

Part 2

Share these happy memories with your partner and ask about his or her memories of:

a wonderful meal you had
drinking your first glass of wine
going abroad for the first time
your first lesson in this class

your first date
smoking your first cigarette
a wedding you've been to
meeting your partner for the first time

Use some of these phrases in your conversation:

I'll never forget...   What do you remember about...?
I'll always remember...   Do you remember...?

39

Part 1

You're going to do several things that may get on your partner's nerves.
Continue doing each thing shown here until you're asked to stop:

*tap your fingers   stare at your partner   doodle   hum a tune
click your tongue*

If your partner's actions get on your nerves, ask him or her to stop by saying:
'Please stop tapping,' or 'Please don't go on staring at me.'

Part 2

Imagine that you're telling your partner about a long walk you once went on.
Ask your partner about his or her walk too.
You had to make several stops on the way and you'll have to explain these:

1st stop: asked the way   4th stop: sheltered from rain
2nd stop: rest   5th stop: another rest
3rd stop: admired the view   6th stop: tea

Your conversation should go like this:

A: Why did you make your first stop?
B: I stopped to pick a flower.
A: I see, and then what?
B: After picking the flower, I went on walking but I soon stopped again.
A: Why did you stop again?

40

-ness

happy	happiness
clever	cleverness
mean	meanness
shy	shyness
kind	kindness
polite	politeness
cold	coldness
selfish	selfishness
neat	neatness
tidy	tidiness
nervous	nervousness

-ity

stupid	stupidity
popular	popularity
original	originality
possible	possibility
responsible	responsibility
equal	equality
certain	certainty
reliable	reliability
inferior	inferiority
superior	superiority
probable	probability
necessary	necessity
sincere	sincerity
mature	maturity
pure	purity
rare	rarity

-ence

violent	violence
patient	patience
confident	confidence
intelligent	intelligence

41

See if you can guess the causes of each event on the right. Your partner knows the correct answers. See if your partner can guess the causes of the events on the left.

Alex is wearing someone else's shoes because he left them outside his hotel room and in the morning...

Bob is looking very happy because he has just got his promotion.

Chris hasn't shaved this morning because he locked himself out of his flat and had to spend the night in a hotel.

David was late for work every day last week for the following reasons:

Mon. alarm clock didn't go off
Tue. car wouldn't start
Wed. traffic hold-up
Thu. ran out of petrol
Fri.   stayed in bed with a hangover

Little Emma is crying.
Frank is very tired.
George has a broken arm.
Hilda was late for work every day last week.

42

warm	cool	angry	calm
nice	nasty	lazy	hard-working
beautiful	ugly	rude	polite
raw	cooked	asleep	awake
wealthy	poor	foolish	sensible
smooth	rough	noisy	quiet
enormous	tiny	arrogant	modest
		tame	wild

gentle	rough	sleepy	wide awake
shy	self-confident	generous	mean
wide	narrow	modern	old-fashioned
deep	shallow	cheap	expensive
fresh	stale	dangerous	safe
absent	present	cowardly	brave
ill	well, healthy	miserable	happy
cruel	kind	difficult	easy

43

Prince Hamlet wants to kill his father's murderer.
In *Remembrance of Things Past* a man remembers his childhood and youth.
In *Goldilocks* a little girl gets lost in a forest and finds a little house.
Popeye (a sailor) gets very strong when he eats spinach.
In *Jaws* a shark terrorises a seaside resort.
King Lear goes mad in the end.

Belinda has curly hair.
Dawn rides a motor bike.
Hazel plays the violin.
Fanny is an airline stewardess.

Anne and you met in London years ago.
Carole used to go out with your brother.
Gwen used to work with your sister.
Elizabeth went to the same school as you.

44

Get your partner to do the sums below on a scrap of paper if necessary, or using a calculator perhaps. Explain step by step what he or she has to do.

2×18 ($= 36$); $+ 3$ ($= 39$); $\div 3$ ($= 13$); $- 4$ ($= 9$);

$\times 7$ ($= 63$); $+ 9$ ($= 72$); $\div 12$ ($= 6$); $- 4$ ('And what's the answer?')

45

break	meat	scene	weight
due	knows	sure	waist
flu	write/Wright	steal	whether
guest	route	tail	weak
whole	piece	through	war

46

Part 1
These are some things you were supposed to do, which you either remembered to do (✓) or forgot to do (✗).
   do the shopping ✓   phone hairdresser ✗   prepare lesson ✓
   collect dry-cleaning ✗   write composition ✗

Find out if your partner did these things that he or she promised to do:
   post letter   buy newspaper   go to bank   get petrol   buy stamps

Use some of these phrases in your conversation:
   Did you remember to...?   I'm afraid I forgot to...   I did remember to...
   I expect you forgot to...   I didn't remember to...   I didn't forget to...

Part 2
Share these happy memories with your partner and ask about his or her memories of:
   a wonderful meal   your first date
   drinking your first glass of wine   smoking your first cigarette
   going abroad for the first time   a wedding you've been to
   your first lesson in this class   meeting your partner for the first time

Use some of these phrases in your conversation:
   I'll never forget... ·   What do you remember about...?
   I'll always remember...   Do you remember..?

47

48

Rewrite this reported conversation in dialogue form, showing only the names of the speakers (Kate and Dan) and giving the exact words they are supposed to have said.

> I tried to find out what Dan was planning to do but he just kept on saying he had no idea. Well, I told him to make up his mind about Lucy. He asked me for my advice so I told him to phone her up and call the whole thing off. He seemed very upset and wanted me to stay with him but I said I couldn't because I had things to do. So I said goodbye and left while he went on trying to persuade me to stay.

49

Ask your partner to react to each of the following promises, threats and offers using the expressions shown on page 59.

If we're not careful someone will...
    scream at us.
    swear at us.
    blame us.
    laugh at us.

If you like I'll...
    give you a present.
    sing to you.
    buy you a drink.
    read my composition to you.
    show you my colour slides.

50

Tell your partner the advantages/disadvantages of the following activities. Where you have advantages to talk about, your partner has disadvantages and vice versa.

```
REASONS FOR NOT KEEPING A DOG:  1 expensive to feed
    2 needs taking for a walk every day
    3 messy and smelly

REASONS FOR GOING ABROAD ON A COACH TOUR:  1 cheaper than independent travel
    2 easy to find friends
    3 always someone to look after you

REASONS FOR NOT GOING TO LIVE ABROAD:  1 you may miss your own country
    2 may be lonely
    3 difficult to make new friends

REASONS FOR BUYING A TELEVISION:  1 many good programmes (e.g. documentaries, films)
    2 news coverage is very good
    3 good, inexpensive entertainment

REASONS FOR NOT OWNING A CAR:  1 journeys quicker by public transport (e.g.
    underground, trains)
    2 expensive to maintain
    3 friends who can give you a lift in their cars
```

51

Imagine that you met an old friend, John, the other day. He was talking to you about his wife, Mary. This is what he said to you.

'I've known Mary for six years now.
I first met her at a New Year's Eve party. In fact it was you who
 introduced us.
We had never met before that.
I was just about to leave when she arrived.
I decided to ask her to dance although I was tired.
We had just one dance before I left the party.
She told me she loved dancing and enjoyed parties very much.
We made a date to meet again a week later.
And we seemed to get on very well and got engaged in the spring.
We got married on November 10.
We went to the Canary Islands for our honeymoon and the weather was glorious.
And we've been happily married ever since – not a single argument in all
 those years. The perfect couple, in fact!'

Report this conversation to your partner, who has been talking to Mary.

52

	-ment		-ion		-ation
announce	announcement	discuss	discussion	admire	admiration
arrange	arrangement	complete	completion	organise	organisation
develop	development	repeat	repetition	hesitate	hesitation
amaze	amazement	suspect	suspicion	educate	education
excite	excitement	oppose	opposition	inform	information
disappoint	disappointment	destroy	destruction	qualify	qualification
embarrass	embarrassment	contribute	contribution	concentrate	concentration
amuse	amusement	decide	decision	vary	variation
treat	treatment	satisfy	satisfaction	apply	application
argue	argument	connect	connection	pronounce	pronunciation
enjoy	enjoyment	permit	permission	explain	explanation
astonish	astonishment	receive	reception	cancel	cancellation
		compare	comparison	expect	expectation
		interrupt	interruption	form	formation

53

Imagine that you and your partner have stocked up with provisions for a camping holiday. Find out what your partner still has left and tell him or her what you have left. Follow this pattern.

A: Have you got any .....**salt**......... left?

B: Yes. How much would you like?   OR   How many .....**packet**......s would you like?

A: .....**Two**........., please.

B: I'm sorry, I've only got .....**one**.........   OR   Here you are!

Things you have run out of	Things you still have left
lemonade	beer (4)
matches	cigarettes (2 pkts)
milk	bread (6 slices)
sugar	honey (½)
toothpaste	chocolate (3)
salt	rice (2)

54

Describe these three uncles to your partner, using these structures:
Both Uncle Alf and Uncle Bert...
Neither Uncle Bert nor Uncle Colin...
Uncle Alf hasn't got either a ... or a ...

ALF   BERT   COLIN

55

proud	pride	efficient	efficiency	friend	friendship
hungry	**hunger**	**warm**	warmth	leader	**leadership**
anxious	**anxiety**	hot	**heat**	accurate	accuracy
safe	**safety**	**high**	height	loyal	**loyalty**
thirsty	**thirst**	deep	**depth**	bored	**boredom**
honest	**honesty**	long	**length**	optimistic	**optimism**
sympathetic	**sympathy**	strong	**strength**	**pessimistic**	pessimism
true	**truth**	**wide**	width	realistic	**realism**
wise	wisdom	**broad**	breadth	brave	**bravery**
angry	anger			**relevant**	relevance

In *Moby Dick* a sea captain is hunting a great white whale.
In *Snow White* a wicked step-mother is trying to kill her step-daughter.
Superman can fly and has other super-human powers.
In *The Day of the Jackal* a man tries to kill the President of France.
Tom, the cat, never manages to catch Jerry, the mouse.
The family in *Dallas* live in Texas.

56

Starting in the bottom right-hand corner, tell your partner the route his or her pen should follow (on page 18) to draw the figures shown here. Make sure your partner draws the figures in exactly the way shown. Don't tell your partner what the drawing is going to show!

57

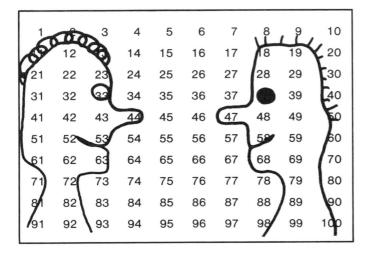

Thanks

I'm very grateful to Sue Gosling, Christine Cairns and Alison Silver for their expert advice, friendly encouragement and sharp eyes. Many thanks also to the teachers at the following schools and institutes, who used the pilot edition and made many helpful suggestions: the Bell College in Saffron Walden, the British Institute in Florence, the British School in Florence, Klubschule Migros in Basle, the Newnham Language Centre in Cambridge and the Sociedade Brasiliera de Cultura Inglesa in Sao Paulo.

The author and publishers are grateful to the authors, publishers and others who have given permission for the use of copyright material identified in the text. It has not been possible to identify the sources of all the material used and in such cases the publishers would welcome information from copyright owners.
Des Moines Art Center, James D. Edmundson Fund, for the painting by Edward Hopper on p. 10; Topham Picture Library for the photograph from *Memory Lane* on p. 11; Thomson Holidays for the map on p. 17; *The Guardian* for the photograph on p. 99; *Citroen Magazine* and Quad Productions Ltd for the photograph on p. 101; *The Observer* for the photograph on p. 106; Times Newspapers Ltd for the photograph on p. 110.

Book design by Peter Ducker MSTD.
Cartoons by Bill Belcher, Noel Ford, Dave McKee, Annie McManus, Dave Parkins and Kipper Williams. Other drawings by Chris Evans, Trevor Ridley and Wenham Arts.